More praise for *Enlighten*

"I am not a religious man. Perhaps my few ┄
Indian missionary boarding school cured n┄ ┄┄┄┄ ┄┄┄┄┄ ┄┄┄ ┄┄ ┄┄┄
fery Paine intimates, even those of us who are 'postreligious' neverthe-
less seek some 'hallowed understanding' of the human condition. Paine
writes such vivid stories about Crestone's eclectic spiritual characters
that, I have to confess, I am charmed beyond belief."

— **Kai Bird,** Pulitzer Prize–winning biographer and author of
The Good Spy: The Life and Death of Robert Ames

"Who knew that among the mountains of Colorado there exists a town
devoted to enlightenment — and boasting twenty-five religious centers, coexisting in perfect amity? How is that possible? In *Enlightenment
Town*, Jeffery Paine takes us on a journey to meets its unforgettable in-
habitants in Airstream trailers, disused mineshafts, and quiet retreats,
across nineteen years. Fascinating, beautifully written, often funny,
sometimes weird — you will love this modern Thoreau."

— **Nigel Hamilton,** award-winning biographer of JFK, Thomas
Mann, Bill Clinton, Bernard Montgomery, FDR, and others
and senior fellow at the University of Massachusetts, Boston

"With warmth, wit, and tenderness, Jeffery Paine introduces us to a remarkable community where the secular and the sacred exist side by side — often
indistinguishably. What is it about a small mountain town in Colorado that
has drawn Buddhists, Christian mystics, Sufis, and a host of other denominations to live together, not with mere tolerance but with something approaching transcendence? Whatever their secret, the residents of what Paine calls a
'Wild West Jerusalem' have lessons for all of us."

— **Tim Folger,** science journalist and series editor of
The Best American Science and Nature Writing

"Whenever we open our hearts with unconditional love and illumine our
brains with boundless wisdom, everything arises as the world of enlightenment. *Enlightenment Town* portrays a true land of Dharma, where this
can happen."

— **Tulku Thondup,** author of
The Healing Power of Mind and *The Heart of Unconditional Love*

"In *Enlightenment Town*, Jeffery Paine takes us on pilgrimage into the heart of what it means to be human. In Crestone, Colorado, home to the world's most religiously diverse community, we venture high into the mountains on sacred vision quests and into cathartic sweat lodges, and join spiritual activists 'on the path.' We leave behind the old stale debate of religion vs. atheism — and belief vs. nonbelief — as we see people living their enlightenment. Joining this pilgrimage, you will be well rewarded."

— **Matteo Pistono,** author of *In the Shadow of the Buddha* and *Meditation*

"*Enlightenment Town* is a lively meditation on the nature of religion and an inquiry into the dynamics of spirituality, articulated with genuine compassion, empathy, and warm, humane humor. A personal and heartfelt exploration of the spiritual, Jeffery Paine's quest situates him in the town of Crestone, high in the mountains of central Colorado, where he interacts with a quirky cast of fascinating characters, spiritual beings from diverse traditions — Hindu, Tibetan Buddhist, Carmelite Christian, Jewish, Taoist, Native American — all of whom have something profoundly in common and each of whom teaches Paine something about the myriad meanings of our relationships with nature and other human beings. As the journey progresses, Paine begins to understand and show us the ways in which everything, no matter how mundane, may be appreciated in some way as sacred."

— **Lee Siegel,** author of *Love in a Dead Language*, *Trance-Migrations*, and other books

ENLIGHTENMENT TOWN

ENLIGHTENMENT TOWN

Finding Spiritual Awakening in a Most Improbable Place

JEFFERY PAINE

New World Library
Novato, California

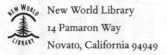 New World Library
14 Pamaron Way
Novato, California 94949

Text design by Tona Pearce-Myers

Library of Congress Cataloging-in-Publication data is available.

First printing, May 2018

ISBN 978-1-60868-574-5
Ebook ISBN 978-1-60868-575-2

Printed in Canada on 100% postconsumer-waste recycled paper

 New World Library is proud to be a Gold Certified Environmentally Responsible Publisher. Publisher certification awarded by Green Press Initiative. www.greenpressinitiative.org

10   9   8   7   6   5   4   3   2   1

*This book is dedicated to
the men and women and children
and mountains and streams
of Crestone.*

God Appears and God is Light
To those poor Souls who dwell in Night,
But does a Human Form Display
To those who Dwell in Realms of day.

— William Blake, "Auguries of Innocence"

Contents

Overture   1

Part I: Town

1. A Dream Awakens   9
2. Where the Hell Am I? A Tour   21

Part II: Religion

3. "Gimme That Old-Time Religion!" Or Is the
   New-Time Better?   33
4. More Religions Than One   67
5. Fewer Than One   89

Part III: Postreligious Varieties
of Experience in Crestone

6. An Ordinary Thursday in Crestone   113
7. A Sacred Relationship to the Natural World?   121
8. Equanimity: Spirituality without the Religion   145
9. The Mind Electric   157
10. When There Is Here and Bitter Is Sweet   173

Finale: Near-Enlightenment Experiences
in Everyday Life

11. The Look of It, the Feel of It   191
12. Nine Rungs Up the Ladder to Enlightenment   203

A Note on Dates   231
Second Dedication   233
About the Author   235

Overture

Far away, remote from anywhere, lies a place that may open an unexpected window onto what it means spiritually to be human. Not all that long before I first strayed there, this high-mountain hamlet had housed but a few score miners' descendants, who when they wanted to eat went out and shot a bear. When I first arrived there, to visit long-unseen friends, I felt I had stumbled onto the set of a budget Western, straight out of *Gunsmoke* or *Bonanza*. Little did I suspect then that that cowboy set, that dot tucked away in the distant mountains, would draw me back again and again and become the place where I felt most at home and would eventually form in my head, without my forcing anything, the book now in your hands.

Back when I first got there, in 1990, I did note the curiosity that a few unusual religious groups — Carmelite, Hindu — had set up shop in this tiny Colorado town. From those small beginnings would soon flower an unprecedented phenomenon. Today the former mining town boasts twenty-five major spiritual centers, representing nearly all the brand names of world religion. Almost all the globe's religions cohabiting practically under the same roof — nothing quite like this had happened before — and there I was, lucky enough to witness it unfolding.

Sadly, I never could live there, not full-time, year-round — a combination of my bad lungs and its too-high altitude — but then the Native American Indians, who once made holy pilgrimages there, thought that landscape too harsh for any two-legged creatures to inhabit. For four-legged creatures, and yes birds too, it was always a peachy place to call home. Oddly, that may be part of its appeal: with its thin mountain air, with few diversions available, with winter practically three seasons out of four, so challenging is living there that having a good ol' time becomes a Darwinian survival mechanism. In that town I discovered that a sense of humor, the spirit of play, is almost a necessity, and eccentricity, instead of being tolerated, is the norm. Who could not help but be attracted to this geosocial nonesuch that counted within a relatively small circumference more visionary, compassionate, offbeat, funny, untamed, and just plain uncategorizable citizens than, square mile for square mile, possibly any other location on the planet? There a religious and a secular zest for experience exist side by side, like good neighbors helping each other out.

This town, Crestone, Colorado, with its larger-than-life characters and wider-than-usual spectrum of permissible behavior, would merit one's curiosity, even were that the whole story. But that the town is also a sort of miniature Wild West Jerusalem offers a rare vantage point and raises an unusual question: What new understanding does beholding the world's various religions all together, each one shedding light on the other, allow us?

Consider this metaphor: If you know five or six — or twenty-five! — languages, you'll see beyond the peculiarities of your native English or Mandarin, understanding how language itself actually works. Likewise for religion and spirituality. Through encountering the town's twenty-five religious groups living side by side, we may begin to fathom what underlies all faiths. And, measuring one against another, we can also gauge how each is adapting to today's changed realities, often trespassing beyond older notions of religion.

Here, in fact, was an author's dream: to write a story never before told. This book is a voyage of exploration — investigation as a mind-heart adventure — into the heart of spirituality. For these townspeople and their sometimes wild tales can help us fathom what it means to live in a period when religion has slipped its millennia-old moorings. Compared to the earlier, seemingly solid ground of God, salvation, biblical morality, sacredness, etc., we have rounded a corner into less certain territory that Rabbi David Cooper, who used to live in this town, called "postreligion."

Commonly accepted matters of faith are now routinely challenged, which leads to this book's heart-queries: Is there a deep, transfiguring human reality, often going by the name *religion*, yet not limited to any or all of the known faiths? From what raw materials, out of what substrata of experience, is a personal transformation mined and refined? To find the answers, must we — with or without the example of Plato and Moses and Siddhartha — descend into the cave and climb the mountain and meditate under the tree once more, this time on our own?

Or could we instead undertake a little jaunt to an unusual

place in the mountains of south central Colorado? *Enlightenment Town* does not catalog contemporary religious denominations so much as explore new possibilities across denominations (and beyond), as brewed in that town's most incongruous melting pot. Shall we pay a visit?

❧

But first I want to anticipate a possible question. If this book treats the broad range of religion today, where in it do we find rabid fundamentalism, religious intolerance, and jihads — those lovely things? It's a reasonable question. For if a self-sacrificing belief in God and faith unquestioned constitute religion, doesn't ISIS put many a good Christian to shame?

Response to the objection: the Inuit supposedly have a hundred words for *snow* and the Bedouin even more for *camel*. As a wider and wilder phenomenon, religion also needs a copious vocabulary of varied names to distinguish its scarcely compatible forms. In *this* book, any group caught being full of hate; bent on violence; racist or misogynistic; and / or killing innocent people is refused admission to the club, i.e., does not fall here within its definition of spirituality. Which is not a problem, for in this town you won't find many — any — fanatics waving bible or flag. The practitioners I knew here — eschewing hatred and harm, accepting those of other faiths as siblings and whenever possible helping them — reveal the better side of religion today.

About religion's dark side, I have inquired. When writing the memoirs of Huston Smith (called the father of comparative religion), I challenged him precisely on this point:

"Huston, your books describe the lovely side of religion, which you know is not the whole story. Why?" "True, guilty as charged," he answered. "I do it for the same reason a class on music concentrates on Bach and Beethoven and not on cacophonous mishmash. That way you can take home something personally valuable from it." Incidentally, Huston dreamed of coming to this town (but was by then too old) to witness all the religions he had so fondly written about coming together in one place. There was no danger of religion blowing up in his face here. To the contrary.

And it won't blow up in your face, either. This is a book written to be useful to (and entertain) the open-minded of any faith. As well as to the one in five Americans who say they are spiritual but not religious, who want examples and companionship for going further, in readable, everyday language that can resonate personally. For here abstract ideals descend to Earth, where they are shown embodied in quirky individuals and amid the raucousness of the common day. To cite one instance: when the esoteric ideas of Eastern spirituality — nonduality, emptiness, "one taste," enlightenment, etc. — migrate westward, they are usually presented in inspiring generalizations. By contrast, in these pages they are depicted on the motley canvas of daily life, as (somewhat) ordinary people in the town use them to relate to one another and to realize a fuller existence for themselves.

To conclude the beginning: Why I Wrote This Book. The world seems to be plunging, with the brakes off, into ever more catastrophic situations. Political realities gone seemingly haywire have left large numbers of people cast out, cast down, wondering where hope is to be found. This was the nonfiction story that I thought I could write that might give my fellow travelers on the planet heart, that might provide imaginative hope and helpful vision. This book cannot pretend to mitigate today's dark turns of events, but its dramatis personae hint at, or more than hint at, how to respond and to live well when circumstances turn adverse. The consolation that, beyond the dictatorship of greed and environmental pillage and alarms of war, there is something else, something better, is a kind of good news, perhaps *now more than ever*.

PART I

TOWN

1. A Dream Awakens

The drowsy, dreaming town was about to wake up, whether it wanted to or not.

Circa half a century ago only a few score old codgers remained in Crestone whose reason for living here was that they were living here. The gold had long run out of this gold-mining town, and boom times had turned into bust times. Should you wonder how the descendants of those old miners supported themselves, the answer is: they didn't. They were living so meagerly that a magnifying glass would scarcely locate their carbon footprint. They inhabited tiny makeshift cabins that they had thrown up themselves from logs they had cut themselves. Their water came from wells they had dug themselves. For food, they went out and shot a deer. If they tired of venison, they shot a bear. Bread was baked in old coffee cans on wood-burning stoves. Their life was rough and hard, and that was just fine with them.

Crestone then half — but only half — resembled other towns in the San Luis Valley of south central Colorado, towns lying on the valley floor as though having fainted of sunstroke. In them forlorn houses lined forlorn streets, often in townscapes so flat they seemed to take place in two dimensions. In such western byways America's Manifest Destiny ran out of gas. Films (*The Last Picture Show*; *Paris, Texas*; *Bagdad Café*) used such desolate towns to evoke American minimalism, the sad barrenness of too little, too lost, too far away.

But located high up — more than eight thousand feet — in the valley's Sangre de Cristo Mountains (which rise to fourteen thousand feet), Crestone was suffused with a kind of nobility that gave it the aura of *somewhere*. Unlike superficially similar small towns, Crestone's terrain has always been a place of Big Dreams — from the Hopi on their vision quests to gold miners on their get-rich quests, from land speculators dreaming of $ signs to today's pilgrims dreaming of a better world. At times their Dream seemed to loom larger than the puny mortals dreaming it, whom it merely used to get itself dreamed.

The Dream has mutated through many incarnations. It is, however, its latest incarnation and the wildest, strangest dream of all that attracts our interest here. This is a story of how that hamlet mutated into something improbable and unclassifiable and without exact parallel elsewhere. Crestone today, with its multiple faiths, is often likened to a miniature, oxymoronic Wild West Jerusalem. But Jerusalem, with its Judaism, Christianity, and Islam, never came close to hosting as many varieties of spirituality, from *A* to *Z* (American Native religions to Zen), as Crestone does. Here, as Eastern spirituality makes its home side by side with traditional Western faiths, it has shaken things up and produced unexpected results — including turning religious differences into a source of social cohesion instead of hostility.

Today the town's twenty-five spiritual centers make it practically a living encyclopedia of the world religions. When you see them all together, what do you see that you didn't when you saw them separate and apart? In the overture, I borrowed an analogy from language: know only one tongue, and you'll mistake it for language itself; know a half dozen, and you may begin to discern their underlying structure and how each one renders reality differently. Likewise with religion. If intimately familiar with several faiths, you may better understand what a religious sense of life is, regardless of its cultural expressions, and what difference, for good or bad, in daily life it can make.

Crestone, with its more than two dozen versions of religion — and in that small dusty Wild West setting — doesn't quite resemble any other place in history. But before we go and inspect it, first a little background: How did such a geographical-cultural-spiritual one-of-a-kind come about in the first place?

History Lessons

Some people, like the Hopi, looked at a landscape and saw something spiritual or *in addition*. One such group of visionaries were the speculators of the 1970s, who looked at Crestone and beheld the summum bonum — filthy lucre, profits, fortune. A land speculation company, the Arizona-Colorado Land & Cattle Co. (AZC), began investing tens of millions of dollars, laying down water pipes and setting up electric lines just outside the town proper, to entice — so their investors hoped — urbanites looking for a better, freer life. The days of the tough old coots who could withstand every hardship, except prosperity, were numbered: capitalism was coming to Crestone.

AZC succeeded in selling a number of lots (when there was no one around to buy them) by setting up tiny sales offices outside army bases, to which was tacked a sign: OWN A PIECE OF COLORADO. $30 DOWN. $30 A MONTH FOR 30 YEARS. A drunken soldier stumbling back to the base might think, "Ah, what the hell" and stumble out of the sales office with three fewer tens in his billfold and a deed to somewhere in New Mexico, no, Colorado. But to sell enough plots of land to make it profitable, AZC faced a small problem — or actually several large ones. Winter in Crestone was most seasons of the year. When winter was eventually over, in blew relentless dust storms that practically kept people prisoners inside. When the dust storms ceased, then came plagues of mosquitoes. In Crestone there were no doctors, no hospitals, no shops, no movies, no entertainment, and (name almost anything else). AZC had a solution to that conundrum, too: they built a golf course. But man cannot live by golf alone. After a few years, the idea of a retirement community in Crestone itself went into retirement, as AZC went bankrupt. And with that ending our story begins.

❧

Three mismatched characters, as though plucked out of three unrelated narratives, now come together to change the face of

Crestone forever. Character number one: a billionaire entrepreneur turned environmentalist. Character number two: a self-appointed local shaman. Character number three: a Danish interior decorator living in New York City. She, number three, would put Crestone on the map and realize there one of the oddest and loveliest dreams in human history. For something new under the sun was taking shape. *The Baca Grande News* — not welcoming this unprecedented development — refused to print her name or report that news. Belatedly, a generation later, here's that news story.

Shamans and interior decorators are not hard to come by; more unusual is a billionaire environmentalist. When Maurice Strong purchased AZC's property assets, including the land around Crestone, his vision for the use of that land...well, he had no vision for it. How could he? He had never seen it or thought about it. The two hundred thousand acres he now owned around Crestone came with the larger two-million-acre Monopoly empire spread throughout the Southwest that he had acquired when AZC went bankrupt. If other entrepreneurs had purchased those two hundred thousand acres, they might have erected a ski resort, or tapped the vast aquifer and piped the water to Denver or Los Angeles, or sold the minerals rights to Halliburton, or leased the land to the military for maneuvers and bomb testing. The mountains are too rugged for commercial skiing, but all those other money-making schemes have been proposed for Crestone. Maurice Strong was at least open to other possibilities.

Unlike Howard Hughes and Donald Trump, who inherited fortunes to fast-start their careers, Strong grew up dirt-poor on the Canadian prairie. Working in the Arctic when barely out of his teens, he learned enough about minerals to make his first million in mining stock. Subsequently, Strong alternated between employment in the private sector, amassing a megafortune — primarily in oil and natural gas — and serving in the public sector. For the Canadian government he oversaw the country's national energy policy, while for the United Nations he supervised the largest famine relief effort in history (in Africa in 1984), and later he masterminded the Rio Environmental Summit of 1992. Already a quarter century ago the *New York Times* was calling Maurice Strong "the Custodian of the Planet." Folks in Crestone were less sure what to call him. The ex-military types living in the Baca land development just outside the town proper were suspicious of Mr. Moneybags barging into their midst. He was a damned foreigner, hence likely to be immoral and depraved. And, sure enough, he arrived in Crestone with a beautiful, *unmarried* female companion on his arm. Strong had planned to headquarter his newly acquired empire in Arizona, but his female companion refused to reside in a city she found as soulless as Phoenix. The couple weighed their options and began exploring their other AZC properties for possibilities. This female companion had, it turns out, a rather unorthodox sense of the possible.

In fact, nothing was more surprising about this billionaire businessman than *her*. Maurice Strong and Hanne Marstrand certainly made the odd couple; their twelve-year difference in age (he was born in 1929, she in 1941) only began the differences between them. Maurice came from the cultureless Canadian prairie; she, from the European high bourgeoisie. He was physically homely and she was beautiful. He was practical-minded, and she spiritually inclined. The *Los Angeles Times* in 1989 titled an article about them "'Mystical' and 'Manifester' Team Up." If Maurice had the financial resources to allow something new to take root in Crestone, it would likely be Hanne who came up with what that something would be.

She had grown up in Copenhagen, believing, the way some believe they are born in the wrong sex, that she had been born in the wrong country. When she read James Fenimore Cooper's *Last of the Mohicans* she thought, "*Those are my people.*" Hanne invented for herself a secret history. "This is my first time around as a white woman," she would say to herself. "For countless generations I was a Native American Indian. Then for countless other generations I was a Tibetan." For a Native American maiden or a pious daughter of Tibet — or even for a proper Danish girl of that era — she certainly behaved inappropriately, becoming (I've been told) one of that new mutant species: the wild teenager, young, daring, beautiful, and saucy.

Hanne relocated to New York in her early twenties, encountering no Mohicans taking scalps but rather Manhattanites drinking manhattans (or martinis). One night Hanne met Maurice at a dinner party, and the rest is — tongues wagging. "It's classic," went the whispers. "Beautiful blonde babe takes rich fool for a ride." Hanne would come home from work to find her apartment filled wall to wall with roses, but Maurice Strong was too shrewd to be duped by a gold digger. For all their differences, theirs was a courtship, a partnership, and later a marriage of mutual appreciation and support. It was thus two seasoned, intimate allies who in 1978 arrived to

inspect the old Crestone ranch, in order to do with the surrounding land...they had no idea what.

What *do* you do with two hundred thousand acres of
semidesert far from anywhere? To a businessman the answer
would be obvious: hire consultants, have a feasibility study
made, conduct market research, and organize a development
oversight committee chaired by accountants. Or, if you are
Hanne, you suspect that this is actually a spiritual question.
To decide the future of the Crestone land, Hanne could imagine only one sensible approach: like an Indian medicine man
she would go on a vision quest. After spending four days
and nights alone in the Sangre de Cristos above Crestone,
as Hanne gazed out at the meadows and nooks and crannies
below, she fantasized a different religion nestled in each of
them. What a cockamamy idea, even she realized.

As Hanne was making her way down the mountain, some
miles away her teenage daughter from an earlier marriage,
Suzanne, was trying unsuccessfully to hitchhike to Crestone.
Finally, some geezer as old as Methuselah slowed his jalopy
and yelled, "Get aboard!" and then plied her with questions
about what a young thing like her was doing in these parts.
When Suzanne told him about her mother, the old fellow
could scarcely contain his excitement. As he dropped Suzanne
off at the ranch house, he quickly scooted out of the car himself. When Hanne answered his banging on the door, he burst
out, "Where you been? I've been waiting for you!"

This man, it seems, had been having his own visions. He
had foreseen a foreign woman coming to Crestone. And that
woman — *You!* he said to Hanne — has a mission to fulfill
here. For a terrible time is coming, war and devastation will
ravage the Earth, and somewhere safe is needed to preserve

the age-old wisdom of humankind. He practically shouted at Hanne: the reason, and the only reason, for your coming here is to establish a refuge for the world's religions. Hanne remembered her vision on the mountain and wondered: Who *is* this man?

By the time he knocked on Hanne's door, Glenn Anderson must have been over eighty years old. What was he? A self-anointed prophet? A shaman? A medium or channeler? He did have one trait in common with all holy persons: he did not work for his own gain. Glenn Anderson lived simply, often sleeping out of doors or in a makeshift cabin so rickety it was like the outdoors indoors. Late in his life he gained some following, principally among hippies, who found his nonmaterialistic idealism and homespun mythology to their liking. Anderson regaled them with stories of how in an earlier incarnation he and the Indian war chief Crazy Horse had been first cousins. Creating a spiritual sanctuary here, he told Hanne that day, was Crazy Horse's vision for the valley. In fact, Anderson went on, Crazy Horse himself was merely the voice for a message far older, one ancient and coterminous with the cosmos. In establishing a habitat for all the world's religions, Hanne would be the medium fulfilling a dream of ancient and universal significance.

Hearing an unkempt old fogy splutter such nonsense, most people would have slammed the door in his face. But Hanne heeded his call, and in the coming years she would devote considerable acreage around Crestone, and seek out representatives of the world's religions to occupy them, to realizing the vision prophesized by Glenn Anderson, or by Crazy Horse, or by the dreaming universe eons ago.

Now that all the principal characters are onstage: the plot — a highly implausible plot, one that would change a half-ghost mining backwater into a setting for the world's religions to come together — is set to unfold.

First there is Maurice. His official residence was now Crestone but his real home was an unending succession of plane flights, from here to there to everywhere. He returned to Crestone bearing unusual souvenirs — the VIPs collected on his travels. Maurice sat on the board of the prestigious Aspen Institute of business, university, and political leaders, and, with his enormous influence, he established the institute's secondary headquarters in Crestone. In those days, the early eighties, you never knew whom you might bump into here. The downtown has about four streets, but walking them you might blink and wonder, Could that really be Henry Kissinger? And that guy, isn't that, you know, the prime minister of Canada, Trudeau? And what about him — Robert McNamara? Yes, it was they.

Then there is Hanne. She was poised to turn a hamlet on the outskirts of nowhere into a center of world religions. In 1980 a front-page article in the *Wall Street Journal* reported that Maurice and Hanne Strong were offering free land in Colorado to traditional religious groups. If spiritual cranks and homemade messiahs don't read the *Wall Street Journal*, somebody must have read it to them. From under rocks and behind trees across the United States sprang yet another bearded oracle or tie-dyed savior heading to Crestone, chanting the mantra, "Gimme, gimme land!"

And then there is the POA. The Property Owners Association was composed largely of ex-military families who, when they moved here, had radically altered Crestone's character. But they now wanted no further change, certainly not the kind Maurice and Hanne were bringing. To the right-wing POA, the little foreigner Strong was barging in with what seemed to them a bunch of damned Reds in tow. If Maurice was bad, they considered Hanne unspeakably worse. She would lure to Crestone weird cults, practicing voodoo and black magic. In the early '80s Hanne received anonymous death threats regularly. Far from appreciating what she was doing, the POA blamed her for everything, short of the weather, and probably that, too.

Yet let a few years fly by, and the metamorphosis has happened; it is a different Crestone once again. The Aspen Institute wives preferred to the majestic mountains of Crestone somewhere where they could get in some good shopping. So, adieu Aspen Institute. Hanne's weird cults turned out to be Christian Carmelites, and later, when they were Hindus or Tibetan Buddhists, they soon shared something with the old-timers there after all. They cared for the community and, equally important, they cared for the land. As each new group here added its flavor to the mix, together expanding the notion of spirituality, the initially resistant old-timers made a discovery: here was religion not as dogmatic moralizing, not as the closed-off churches of their past, but as a more multidimensional milieu in which even nonbelievers could live and thrive. The old town still looked the same, as earthy and folksy as ever, but the shutters of possibility were thrown open, and the unimaginable became imaginable.

When, for example, in the early nineties outside corporate interests planned to drill the aquifer and drain the water table, wreaking environmental havoc, it was unthinkable that with their money, power, and influence they could be stopped. But the ecologically minded members of the new religious groups, joined by old Crestonians and ranchers and farmers from across the valley, voted to tax themselves for funds to legally oppose the mammoth corporations. When against the odds they eventually won their impossible David-versus-Goliath battle, one old conservative rancher from the valley, elated by the results, joked to a man from here, "You know, you weirdos from Crestone are all right." The man joined in the joke and laughing, replied, "Yep, our alien guides from outer space instructed us to save the land."

Yes, even without the alien guides, it was implausible. Hanne's (Glenn Anderson's / Crazy Horse's / the dreaming universe's) vision for Crestone came to fruition. Mecca, Jerusalem, Bodh Gaya…and now little Crestone? In that small geographical compass twenty-five different spiritual groups — Christian, Tibetan Buddhist, Hindu, American shamanic, Sufi, Zen — have set up shop, living neighbor to neighbor, providing a unique picture or insight into spirituality today. A mining and ranching town on the fringe of nowhere, headed for extinction, became instead a twenty-first-century microcosm of the world's religions. Toward the end of his life William Faulkner looked up from his astonishing body of work and wondered: Where did it all come from? Unlike Faulkner, Hanne looks at her unusual creation and finds it not surprising at all. She merely thinks: "Of course it happened. It had to happen."

2. Where the Hell Am I? A Tour

S uppose you were set down here blindfolded, could you guess — by the sounds, the temperature, the air quality, the felt speed of people passing by — roughly where you had landed? The temperature seems a bit cold for the time of year, since either in winter you stand deep in snow or in August the nights sink into the fifties. There is clue number one. The air inhaled has a fresh, dry exhilaration but, shortchanged a few molecules of oxygen, you cannot quite take in enough of it. Second clue, you are at a high altitude. Your ears strain to catch any telltale sounds, but how peculiar, there are none, no hum, rumble, or din to be heard. A wind does sigh through the trees, and an unidentifiable bird faintly cries, but where are the screeching alarms of ambulances, the coughing of leaf blowers, and the ear-piercing squeals of trucks backing up? Quietness is a scarcely obtainable commodity in the noise-polluted twenty-first century, and curious about how you landed in such a hotbed of silence, you rip off the blindfold. And then...a multiple-choice question. When you tear off the blindfold you see you are:

a)   where the following story gets under way
b)   in a Western, possibly Colorado township
c)   nowhere, or nowhere you would want to be
d)   on sacred terrain
e)   not on sacred terrain
f)   in Tibet

If you answered (f), you are wrong — but not obviously wrong. Set against Himalayan-like mountains, the terrain here is a doppelgänger for parts of Tibet. Like a village in old Tibet, the town sits at a high-plain-like altitude (eight thousand feet), abutted by even higher mountains (fourteen thousand feet), and overlooking a vast, seemingly empty valley (160 miles across). Tibet bares the nickname Land of Snows, and here, too, it can snow for months, alternating with dazzling blue skies, followed by a summer warmed by a blazing sun. And as in Tibet, Crestone's terrain may be inhospitable to much in the way of development, but that very inhospitality makes it hospitable for retreats, monasteries, devotional practices, and solitary introspection. When the two most venerated lamas of Tibet visited Crestone they couldn't get over it. "This is a place where Tibetan Buddhism can survive!" exclaimed one (the 16th Karmapa), and marveled the other (Dilgo Khyentse), "Many beings will become enlightened here!" Indeed, for some Buddhist practitioners today, Crestone is a New World annex of Old Tibet, but, even so — look on any map — if you answered (f) you flunked the quiz.

All the other answers above have some claim to being right. For most unblindfolded gazers the answer would be (c), Crestone is nowhere (nowhere they have ever heard of; nowhere with touristic attractions). Crestone lies hours away from any major airport. From that airport (either Denver or Albuquerque), you start out on busy highways, then drive down ever less crowded ones, and finally down a two-lane road, and when the road runs out and you can't go any farther: Welcome to Crestone. In recent years the town has gained some reputation for its religious centers, which lures some tourists wanting to behold that spiritual extravaganza. Did their GPS go haywire? As an excuse for a downtown all they find is a post office, a few small businesses, and some empty buildings, situated on two north-south-running streets crisscrossing two east-west-running streets — negligible man-made scratches in a forlorn expanse of eternally arid real estate. (The various religious centers lie tucked away in the mountains, unobservable from the town.) Hanne Strong's aristocratic mother visited from Denmark and took one glance at this — by her European standards — uncultured backwater, and she did not need a second. When informed that someone was writing a book about the town, she snorted, "It better be titled *One Day Here Is Enough*."

To get the lay of the land, let's take a drive on the land surrounding the town (the Baca, where most Crestonians live), which stretches mile after mile across prairie-like semi-desert. We might be on the set of every other cowboy movie ever made. Yup, boys and girls, we're out West. Or are we?

The houses you pass in that expanse form a crazed United Nations of domestic architecture. The first house is New England clapboard, but the next one you come to is Spanish adobe, followed by a log cabin; the one after that could be a futuristic Hobbit-hole, and a mile down the road is an alien spacecraft-like dwelling. On the right you ride by an Oriental palace, and on the left, why, look — a mound of dirt that got overly ambitious. After a while you ask yourself, What planet am I on? Crestone has no building code, which is what first drew ornery mavericks here, after the gold ran out.

Driving back into town we pass old-fashioned Americana, a plain old wooden Baptist church. I once slowed down to read its sign, which announced that Sunday's sermon: CHRIST'S ERECTION. Whoa! If Jesus were a man as well as God, he could have had boners, I guess, but when had the Baptists gotten so frisky? The sign, it turns out, had originally read *Christ's Resurrection*, until some mischief-makers got hold of it. (A sense of humor substitutes here for the commercial entertainments available elsewhere.*)

Indeed, the real hero of this book may not be any individual, lovely as he or she may be, or spiritual group, interesting as they are, but the land. Our hero cannot speak for itself, but others are ready to speak for it, to say what living in such a momentous landscape means. Sister Kaye compares her Carmelite monastery here, Nada Hermitage, with their monasteries elsewhere: "At the Nova Scotia monastery we experience God through beauty. In Ireland we sense God through the people. Here in Crestone we know God mainly through nature." Granted that all Earth is sacred, Walter Roan, an

---

* An earlier sign on the Baptist marquee had read: GOD'S FAVORITE WORD IS COME! When a couple, Mark Jacobi and Chris Canaly, decided to get hitched, they lewdly draped themselves over the sign and used that lascivious photo on their wedding invitation — *COME*. The Baptist minister's wife then ran into Chris at the grocery store and, innocent of the sexual meaning of the word, gushed, "You used our sign on your wedding invitation. Aren't you just the sweetest, sweetest people on earth!"

old Cree medicine man visiting Crestone, was asked, "What makes the land here especially so?" "Where the land is open and vast, when there's water underneath [referring to the aquifer], and wind blowing across into the mountains, there is spirit and there is no place for the spirit to go then but up," Roan answered. "Here everything rises."

Let's rise ourselves, and climb partway up one of those fourteen-thousand-foot peaks, and from there, looking down, obtain a last atavistic view of lost, virgin America. Below, the valley spreads out seemingly without end, and from this height it appears unscarred by human history or habitation. It is no Garden of Eden, for it is not verdant or rich in luxuriant vegetation. Rather, imagine the harsher landscape that Adam and Eve stumbled out into afterward, where the taunting wind sighed, "It is not too late. Something else there yet may be. Let us try once again."

Crestone: Sacred Turf?

Spirituality is Crestone's cash crop. Imagine that every genre of Hollywood film got spliced by a crazed editor into the same surrealist movie. A religious version of that movie — mixing together holy hermits, a bearded rabbi, monasteries, ashrams, crucifixes, goddess statues, Buddhist stupas, a Middle Eastern ziggurat — is playing daily in Crestone, with no need for projector or screen. Hindu nuns in saris umpire at the local baseball games. At the Christmas Mass at the Carmelite monastery, whole rows get taken by Buddhist monks in their flowing draperies. It's like a League of Nations of spirituality, assembling five continents and three thousand years of religious history. This — the cohabiting of so many of the world's religions, all breathing down each other's necks — has never happened before.

What would you like to do? Sweat it out in a Native American sweat lodge? Be *frum* (devout) at the Yom Kippur services in the old 1880s schoolhouse? Meditate in an old mine shaft, which serves as your hermit's cave? Twenty-five religious groups populate Crestone, but the most important one may be the twenty-sixth, the culminative effect of all of them together, which you need not attend services to be part of. Elsewhere spirituality is the Sunday or Sabbath singularity of the week; here it *is* the week. You can hear the hum of religion, even when you are not listening. When those you bump into at the post office are practitioners, when it's what you see all around you and take in without even trying, when it's in the jokes told, even as a nonbeliever you can be an uninfected carrier of spirituality.

But is Crestone itself — is anywhere — sacred land? The answer to such a question could influence how we treat our natural surroundings, whether we exploit or preserve them. Let's explore three possible answers as to whether Crestone is sacred turf.

1. *No.* Some folks here spill their fantasies over the landscape like a can of overturned paint. Some have even moved to Crestone expecting that living in a spiritual place would ameliorate their problems — a marriage gone sour or unmanageable children. Harsh remote surroundings, where diversions and distractions are few, however, can actually make those troubles worse. Many arrive bearing a bundle of hopes and

later leave, forgetting to take that bundle with them. "Crestone's one renewable resource," Kizzen Laki, the newspaper editor, jokes, "is disillusioned visionaries."

2. *Yes.* That *yes* once would have been the Native Americans' unqualified response. Although no one could live in such a harsh, charged environment, or so they believed, the Hopi and the Ute and the Navajo undertook pilgrimages to these mountains, regarding them as a spiritual entity. Before horses were reintroduced into America, travel in this high valley meant inching across it, allowing the landscape to migrate inside you. Here, where Earth heaves up almost to touch heaven, they found a fine place to meditate, to fast, and to pray, and the best place of all to die. (With the winds blowing against the mountains, Walter Roan said, the departed's spirit could only go up.)

3. *Yes and no* (or *no and yes*). Einstein asserted that for an intelligent adult there exist only two possibilities: either that nothing is miraculous or that everything is. Two construction workers in Crestone, Jack Siddall and Pattison Kane, decided to work only on sacred buildings, and with that decision carpentry lost its tediousness. Pattison is now working on a Buddhist temple high up in the mountains, and as he reflects on the temple's purpose and all who will benefit, he gets excited, as though each detail he carves or paints is a holy icon. When some residents claim that the Sangre de Cristos are divine handiwork, that belief may impose on a matter-of-fact piece of physical geography lustrous associations and cloak it in an intangible aura, whether real or imagined.

About whether or not Crestone is holy ground, why have so many great Tibetan masters in exile made a beeline to here, I have wondered, when it's so off the beaten track, hard to get to, and offering little in the way of potential students or influence? This is the answer told to me: Centuries of Native Americans on sacred pilgrimage to Crestone have seeded the ground here with blessings and infused the atmosphere with their lingering prayers. How could anyone evaluate a statement like *that*? Besides, it only pushes the question back a notch in time: Why, then, did so many great Native Americans make a beeline here?

Perhaps what drew them is that in few other places have hardship and majesty married each other so well as they have here. With its tall mountains on the right and a vast valley on the left (or if you're standing the other way around, then the other way around), majestic Crestone certainly is. But it can be hard to live here. In spring unrelenting winds howl for weeks on end — saturated with agricultural chemicals blowing up from the valley — and can make you half-crazed. In winter you can be snowed in for weeks and, when snows stop, the black ice on the roads can still keep you housebound. At such times it is just you and the mountains and vast, empty space — no way and nowhere to hide — and everything within you may rise up and you will have to meet it as never before. "Crestone is not the best place to come if you want pleasurable experiences," one practitioner here (Esteban Hollander) observed. "But a great, great place if you want to 'wake up.'"

You cannot buy a digital gauge on eBay to measure the spirituality of a place. Perhaps the only measure is whether it makes its citizenry consistently more thoughtful, more generous, and lighter and kinder. Crestonians, in my unofficial census, often do display more helpfulness, open-mindedness, and playfulness than most other locals I know. I am writing this book, hoping that vicariously it might do something similar for some reader (and for me as well).

And with that thought, we can supply the answer to the multiple-choice quiz earlier in this chapter. It is (a): where the story now gets under way.

PART II

RELIGION

3. "Gimme That Old-Time Religion!" Or Is the New-Time Better?

About religion, that most controversial of subjects, one question never goes away: Is religion a good thing, or is it bad, bad, bad?

The answer to this question must wait in line, however, while a prior one gets answered first. Since so many contrary practices go by that name, what is the common denominator — if there is one — that makes them all religion? My Sunday school teachers could have dispatched that question with ease. Religion for them was God "above" and moral behavior "below," and *where* to find it would be inside a church or temple and *when* would be Sunday or Easter (or if you're Jewish, Saturday and Yom Kippur). Now one could almost weep for such innocent simplicity, when God looked like Michelangelo's portrait of him on the Sistine Chapel ceiling. Faith back then was as simple as believing what the Bible or your clergyman said. And now? Now there are books bearing titles like *Religion without Belief* and even *Religion without God*, and in them God floats in a vapory cloud of abstraction. Rilke described God as a direction and Rabbi David Cooper, formerly of Crestone, said *God* was a verb. And if you are being religious at a Mass or a Shabbat service, what are you when you are grocery shopping or carrying out the garbage or texting?

Crestone is a made-to-order laboratory for investigating such matters, for here the old, the new, and the strange of religion jostle side by side.

Christianity

Father Dave Denny, a Carmelite monk in Crestone, was asked an unusual question, one he hadn't heard before. A well-mannered tourist from Japan had traveled to America, and to understand this country before he embarked on his journey, he had read its holy book, the Bible. To this Japanese Buddhist, the Judeo-Christian book contained everything — mythology, morality, poetry, history — everything except one thing: Where, he wondered, where was the religion in it? For him religion was not miracles or moral commandments but working with your mind to transform negative emotions, to obtain enlightenment. Father Dave had to laugh, saying, "No, if you don't think this is what religion is, then you may miss it in the Bible."

To witness traditional old-fashioned Christianity, if not Crestone then the terrain around it is the right place to come to. "Seek and you shall find, knock and it shall be answered," the Bible says. I didn't have to. Christianity knocked on my door in Crestone one afternoon. Woke me up from a world-class nap. Or was I still dreaming? At the door stood two unfamiliar African American women, more properly attired than anyone I'd ever seen in Crestone. Through the screen I wondered whether they could see me, for I was wearing only my underwear. Probably not — they weren't running away, screaming in horror. In my groggy state I was slower than I should have been to identify these unfamiliar women. Jehovah's Witnesses.

They were spreading the Good Word. Spreading it all the way from Fullerton, California, since the nearest Jehovah's Witness church around here, the one in the town of Center, had only thirty members, too small to do much spreading. To bring the most valuable gift of all to endangered souls, those two brave women willingly endured personal sacrifices without complaint. Instead of complaining, they panted: the high altitude of Crestone was obviously a trial to their lungs, and that wasn't the only trial. They had, unprepared, wandered into the land of — what were folks around here, Buddhists or Hindus? Everybody, they reported, was so polite to them, everyone courteous, yet they sensed they were not making much headway.

I took this as a challenge; I would make them feel good about sojourning among pagans. And it *was* a challenge. After reading sections from Revelations, they asked if I could envision that a time will come when there shall be no more death. "You know, I'm really not sure." They foretold of the coming era when men and beasts shall dwell together in perfect harmony. I kept silent, not blurting out, "Better be soon, while there's still some other species left." Why was my (silent) reaction so churlish? If what they were describing was religion — man and beast and God all one in the immortality of forever — what's not to like? And how their vision sustained them: aging, illness, misfortune, and dying will likely shatter them less than the flu does me. Why didn't I convert on the spot, right there in my skivvies?

I found a clue as to why later that night. There was a party to welcome back Tsoknyi Rinpoche,* Crestone's brilliant and funny Tibetan teacher, from his teaching and travels. At the party Tsoknyi told about a wealthy Indian woman who had adopted his book *Carefree Dignity* as her personal bible and would stop at nothing, certainly not his wishes, to get him to come teach in India. "She is a tough lady," Tsoknyi said, "but kind-tough, which is okay, not nasty-tough."

"Tough lady?" challenged a woman at the party, obviously a tough lady herself, who suspected Tsoknyi of harboring antifeminist stereotypes. "Pray, tell us, Rinpoche, what you mean by *tough lady*."

"A tough lady, like a tough man," he answered, nonplussed, "is somebody who rolls over everything to get what she wants. Including other people. She talks, you listen."

I was reminded of those mild women of Fullerton, every inch proper and demure, who were undercover tough ladies. They had talked and I had listened. Since all the Buddhists hereabouts puzzled them, I suggested that they might want to read Thich Nhat Hanh's *Living Buddha, Living Christ*, which explains Buddhism in terms sympathetic to Christianity. But they obviously had no interest, and that merely begins the list of things uninteresting to them. Including me. I was a generic Homo sapiens container, and as such suitable for filling with Christianity, Jesus, and God. If Jesus was the Way, I was just

---

* *Rinpoche* is not a name but a Tibetan honorific for a (supposedly) conscious reincarnation.

in their way, the next person in line to receive their announcement of the Truth.

Though not Crestone itself, much of Colorado belongs to the Christian Kingdom. I entered that kingdom two days later, when I drove to the High Valley Stampede, Colorado's oldest rodeo, in Monte Vista. That small town had swung into the saddle for the weekend and was enjoying itself immensely. From kids with chili-cheese fries to grandpas with oxygen tanks, everybody there knew one another. One event of sweetness was a lamb-riding competition in which pre-kindergartners held on for their dear little lives to bucking lambs. Another competition pitted against one another the fire departments from the neighboring towns, racing to rope, and put enormous ladies' panties on, an indignant heifer.

But evidently one more item was required for that rodeo to be complete. The Messiah. The rodeo's emcee, a beefy dude in cowboy duds, straddling an enormous horse, kept announcing through his hand mike, "Being good is good. But not good enough. Friends, recognize Jesus Christ as your savior. He was God's greatest gift to us, so let us be our greatest gift to him." I did not disagree, of course, but maybe it was the heat or my overindulgence in chili-cheese fries, for I had no idea what he meant. The most opaque words open to various interpretation — *God, savior, our gift to him* — were tossed around like tangible objects, like *rope* or *saddle*.

The emcee's inspirational message was like a coded signal, meant for those who already knew the code. I looked around: What did Christianity have to do with any of this? Bareback bronco riding is as daring a feat as exists in sports, but to what does it correspond in the New Testament? The

Jehovah Witnesses' promise of God's creatures living in harmony rules out rodeos in heaven. For a moment the rodeo vanished and in its place was organized cruelty to animals. A minute later, though, I got caught back up in its excitement.

Half a century ago, when I was a boy, the future of Christianity was thought to lie with thinkers like Kierkegaard, Reinhold Niebuhr, and Paul Tillich, who used the meeting of Christianity and modernity to deepen our understanding of both. But the mainstream churches whose members once read such theologians are increasingly empty; rather, the pews are filled with fundamentalist tough ladies and gents like the Fullerton Jehovah's Witnesses and the rodeo emcee. I decided, when I got back to Crestone, to meet a different kind of Christian, a "Crestone Christian."

If that was my goal, I was told several times, Father Dave Denny was my man. "Father Dave," so said the English filmmaker Mark Elliott (who will figure prominently in the narrative later), "he is what a Christian should be." That was high praise, for I was surprised that Mark thought anybody should be a Christian.

I made some inquiries about this Father Dave, and if what people said was true, then he is that seeming impossibility: a completely good man. People who have known him for years cannot recall his ever once being mean-spirited. The worst display of temper anyone recalls is when an irritating woman was being willfully obtuse and Father Dave burst out, "Jeepers, Sharon!" Furthermore, so I was told, Father Dave was a completely devout Christian but not bound by what that had meant in the past. Hearing such reports, I did want to meet him — perhaps a new kind of Christian for a new century?

To seek out a sage, in mythological tales, the pilgrim must wind his or her way through unmarked trails, panting and stumbling, up to the top of a mountain. Father Dave, in fact, lives high up on a mountainside just outside Crestone. Since the chances of my successfully winding and finding were practically nil, Father Dave drove down to drive me up. I was greeted by a slim, trim, neat, bearded man, perhaps in his midfifties. He drove me to something equally trim and neat, his nine-hundred-square-foot house, a dot in that high-desert emptiness. A perfect cabin for retreat and contemplation. Father Dave hardly resides there as in a monastic cell, though, being busy in the world: he runs the Desert Foundation, promoting the desert as a source of spirituality; he serves as the chaplain at a distant college; he travels to raise money for a relief and development agency (Cross Catholic Outreach) that brings clean water, nutritional food, and shelter to the Earth's downtrodden; and he takes care of his mother, who has Alzheimer's.*

Father Dave's story begins in a practically pastoral idyll in a bygone America. To say that Kokomo, Indiana's thirteenth-largest "city," resembled a Norman Rockwell small town sounds dismissive, but it did look like a Norman Rockwell painting. Farmers wore bibbed overalls to church, and their wives, starched spotless aprons. Cocooned in a large loving family, young Dave assumed that basic human goodness was a fact of life.

---

* Late in the time span this book covers, Dave's mother died.

Religion in midcentury America, unlike today, occupied a fairly marginal place, for most restricted to Sundays and holidays. But then came the spiritual-questing sixties (which occurred mainly in the seventies). In the heady spirit of those times, Dave enrolled in a college course about a book largely unfamiliar to him: the New Testament. During that course he learned all sorts of surprising things, such as that there were still monks. In the twentieth century! Dave read about one monk, named Thomas Merton, who observed monastic vows yet was fully engaged in the issues of his time. If, in the spirit of the sixties (seventies), Dave decided to experiment by going on a group retreat, it was hardly odder then than going to the Apple store would be today.

At the retreat the other participants vied to sit next to him. Though Dave was funny and told jokes, and his fellow retreatants sensed him a pleasant person to be around, there was something more, a deep peacefulness, in him. Inspired by the retreat, Dave entertained a romantic hypothesis: to live fully, either become a monk, embracing a spiritual world, or be like Zorba the Greek, exuberant in this earthy one. The person leading the retreat, Father William McNamara, was a revelation to him: a monk *and* wild — a Zorba of faith. A few years later, inspired by Father William's example, Dave himself took vows.

At his vow taking, Dave expressed gratitude to someone for a life-changing experience that had brought him to that moment. It caused surprise, especially at a Catholic ceremony, for the one Father Dave thanked was the Buddha. He appreciated that the Buddha emphasized experience over beliefs and that Buddhism itself required no more otherworldly metaphysics than did an experiment in physics: do A, and B will follow. Do meditation, and your mental world will be transformed. He wondered how many Christians could say the same about the effects of church attendance. Earlier Dave had gone on a Buddhist Vipassana retreat, and its effects surpassed his every expectation, but must he, he wondered, swallow Buddhism's strange and unfamiliar pill? Or could he have the same (or better!) experience through Christianity? There was one way to find out. His taking monk's vows that day was that way.

Father Dave thus became a Christian, but not one out to convert anyone else to his beliefs. As for our being God's favored people, he says, this belief charges a Christian's life with dignity — but he doubts any God's validity who would choose one people over another. He can even imagine someone forsaking Christianity for Christian reasons: because it has become too much rote assent, a form of idol worship. Such an attitude will hardly ignite faith-based wars or allow shady politicians to hide behind a Bible. Father Dave's measure of whether Christianity — or for that matter, any religion — is at work in your life is simple: Has it made you more alive, more loving, more capable of relationship?

Is there a limit to such ecumenical open-mindedness? For there are differences too deep to be simply waved away. In Buddhism nothing is permanent, while in Christianity one's soul (which also doesn't exist in Buddhism) is durable unto death — and beyond. Another difference: in Christianity, God is the creator of the universe; in Buddhism, no God, and no creation, either. I asked him, "How would you, Father

Dave, go about reconciling Buddhism and Christianity, with their contrary claims?"

"I don't. I can't," he answered mildly. "Each may be true, while you're thinking about it, especially if thinking about it makes you for that moment a better person." In the old Judeo-Christian worldview, he said, each person was considered a container, and each container/person could be filled with only one religion. He proposed a newer, more accurate metaphor: a map. Everyone has inside him or her a map or blueprint of all spiritual possibilities. Some people stay within the shaded area of the religion in which they were born, never venturing into the unknown white spaces. Still, the map or predisposition of other religious potentialities is latent within them.

We were sitting in Father Dave's postage stamp–size kitchen, overlooking an endless, arid landscape of such ancient timelessness as to make the words *infinity* and *eternity* almost palpable. We drank tea and speculated about great matters — a not unpleasant way to pass the afternoon. We were bound to eventually come around to the subject of Jesus — bound to, because of course I brought it up.

"We could be entering a new era," Father Dave speculated, "in which, perhaps for the first time, we are beginning to comprehend fully who or what Jesus was." What a treat! Two thousand years passed before me, as it were, in four successive blinks of the eye — the whole history of Christianity in four movements. It begins with the period of *Christ*, when during his lifetime and for three centuries thereafter disciples attempted on their own — without the dictates and dogma of an official Church — to figure out who Jesus was and what his relation to the godhead was. This period yielded to *Christendom*, when in 380 CE the faith became the Roman Empire's state religion, and for the next millennium earthly power and divine authority were practically interchangeable, each underwriting the other. Then in the Renaissance and Reformation commenced what Father Dave called by the familiar name *Christianity*, when it was no longer the official state religion yet Christ-as-God still shaped people's thinking, the divine component of their overall worldview. But now, he said, we, or at least many Christians, are entering a new era of faith.

"As for a name for this new era," Father Dave suggested, "it might not be *Christianity* but *Christ-ness.*" In it Jesus may be less a God to worship and more a model of how to incarnate divinity within yourself. He elaborated. "We have brooded too long on God's omnipotence, which may not get us very far, and not enough on Christ's love and perfect compassion, which radiates in us, too." Before my eyes Father Dave was shifting the locus of Christianity / Christ-ness from orthodoxy to orthopraxy, from creed to experience. "Even now a consciousness resembling Jesus's," he said, "may be coming to fruition in ever more souls."

When I mentioned the filmmaker Mark Elliott — a good man who was at times called "the king of Crestone" and is Buddhist to the core — Father Dave said that when looking at Mark he saw Christ. If I had Father Dave's breadth of vision, would I have not simply been talking about Jesus with him but sensing his presence as well?

Later, after Father Dave dropped me off, something about that afternoon struck me. He had not made any argument in

favor of Christianity. Though his Christian faith is everything to him, Father Dave voiced no claim for its superior-
ity. Does that "noble silence" — that spiritual humility, that
lack of religious jingoism — rare in the epoch of Christianity,
characterize a new era of Christ-ness?

But why was Father Dave living all by his lonesome up in
a mountain cabin and not — for he is a monk — in a monastery? He originally came to Crestone to join a Carmelite
monastery, Father William McNamara's Nada Hermitage,
erected in the high desert's void and vastness. The handsome
monastery so architecturally suits the high desert as to practically materialize out of it. In its chapel glow two stained-
glass windows depicting not the apostles but a black slave,
a downtrodden woman, a suffering Vietnamese, a wounded
animal, and other beings in travail, to remind the monks and
nuns why they are here: to pray for and aid whoever sorrows.
Indeed, the Carmelites quietly help people here in need, without broadcasting it. For Father Dave the years rolled by at
Nada, the work went well, the monastics dwelt in harmony
together, all was of a loveliness. Until...

Until it was discovered that the head of the hermitage,
Father William, hardly the chaste monk he presented himself
as, had seduced one nun after another. And this was the man
who, if a monk and a nun at Nada fell in love and renounced
their vows in order to marry, exiled them and pronounced
them anathema. "At least," Hanne Strong commented about
his misconduct, "it wasn't with children." Father Dave did

not have the luxury of such detachment. He had worked closely with Father William for thirty years, and what he once thought true now seemed a sham. Father Dave's life work, his vocation, his belief in inherent goodness, everything he had trusted — the whole edifice — crumbled in an instant.

His days now began not with a psalm book in the chapel but with the question, "Can I get out of bed?" His body was shaking, he could barely eat. Barely talk. He felt that if he remained in the monastery he was doomed and that if he left the monastery he was doomed. Besides, how would he support himself (not many ads run "Freelance Monk Wanted")? The chaplain of Colorado College tried to encourage Father Dave, telling him he had much to look forward to. Dave understood the words separately — *me...look forward... something good* — but how did they apply to him?

Needing to get away somehow, Dave rented Mark Elliott's retreat cabin above Crestone. "Just one thing," Mark joked. "Please don't find God in a Buddhist cabin." It felt good to be in a Buddhist atmosphere again and be reminded of its basic teaching of impermanence, that nothing, including his despair, lasts forever. That thought deepened into: if I want to be true to the essence, I may have to leave the form behind. The form had been his work at Nada with Father William, but the essence was faith in a goodness despite transgressions, at once within and independent of circumstances. With that realization, Father Dave moved to his new home, that cabin high on the mountainside, where the timelessness and impersonal emptiness of the desert — an experience of wordless existence beyond categories, beyond personal suffering

— helped heal him. His was a Christian kind of story, of one returned from the dead.

A few weeks after visiting his cabin, I stumbled on a clue as to how Father Dave can wear his deeply felt Christianity so lightly. The clue came, oddly enough, from a Buddhist teacher who was visiting Crestone. During the retreat he was leading, he said — it sounded odd, coming from a religious teacher — that leaving religion behind creates a paradise for certain people.

This gentle teacher, Anam Thubten, described three levels to the religious life. The first level is belief: one assents to an ideal. At this level devotees "believe," but their belief does not necessarily determine, or even much interfere with, their customary behavior (nor are they ruined if the belief turns out not to be true). This is religion as ideology, personal comfort, and grand thoughts.

The next level, Anam said, is religion itself. And religion is a very serious business. You have a lot to think about now: What's the morally right thing to do? Is it in accordance with divine law? Do I have a good conscience? You are shouldering grave responsibilities — enough to hunch you over as you bear so much dogma, duty, and goodness. It's a 24/7 job, with good works instead of vacations; it's a school in which ethical satisfactions take the place of recesses, and the homework assignment is for all eternity.

The third level of religion comes after that, on the other side of Bible reading, temple attendance, and good works.

Religion is not left behind, but your way of living now allows its truths or insights to materialize on their own. Sacred manuals are no longer necessary; you seem to know without trying to know. After continual striving and duty rendered, finally after age sixty, Confucius said, he could do what he wanted without going against the path. (How such a harmonious state of being comes about is investigated in part 3 of this book.) Father Dave appears today to be that kind of almost effortless Christian. As for Jesus's teachings, they are no longer found only in scripture: effortlessly, automatically, they arise in his thoughts to meet whatever the situation is, and opening his eyes wide, he sees the teachings on display all around him. First thing after waking, Father Dave enters into contemplation, which is deeply gratifying, but for him the experience feels not all that different from when he cuts firewood or goes into town for groceries. Everything has become liturgy.

Does Father Dave — open-minded and inquisitive, undogmatic, recognizing his religion's kindredness to other faiths — augur a better future for humanity?

Possibly not. Christianity is growing by leaps and bounds, particularly in Latin America and Africa, but often it is not Father Dave's version but a narrower faith, shuttered against other possibilities, damning all forms of religious expression except itself. Dave attended a conference in the Northwest, where he was admiring a magnificent totem pole, a wondrous expression of folk art, full of potent mythic symbols, when a

Christian delegate from the developing world sneered, "We should burn it to the ground. It's the handiwork of Satan."

Still, the future may not be solely a question of numbers, of statistical majorities. The religious cast of mind, as noted, wears bifocals: it sees the relative *and* the absolute, or the historically conditioned *and* the unconditional, or the daily *and* the eternal. From that double perspective, the *quality* of a Father Dave's open-mindedness and open-heartedness may spiritually outweigh the *quantity* of intolerance elsewhere. A relevant story in the Bible: in the sinful city of Sodom, if one honest man could be found, God would spare the whole metropolis. And in the town of Crestone — since we are not even through with this chapter — we may find a few other folks like Father Dave who lace their faith with honesty and generous understanding.

Buddhism

The fire scorches you yet suffuses no light, so your dim eyes cannot distinguish day from night, and it is always night.... The fire, burning hot like the sun, was created for no other purpose than your torture, the just reward for your shameless and unspeakable sins.*

To go from sampling the above hellfire and damnation sermon — once an ornament of Catholicism — to Father Dave's accepting wide vision is like emerging from a claustrophobic cell into fresh daylight. Do other religions traverse a similar arc, too, from a somber older moralism into a more

---

*   Paraphrased from James Joyce's *Portrait of the Artist as a Young Man.*

user-friendly contemporary ethos? What would, for example, a modern Buddhist be like?

Beginning in the late 1960s the first Tibetan Buddhist gurus arrived in America. Even if they had spoken English (which usually they didn't), their teachings would still in effect have been in Tibetan. For example: "Consider that every sentient being in the universe was at one time your mother" was a traditional teaching given in many talks. At one talk, restless after hearing that platitude one more time, first in Tibetan and then in English, I did the math: millions of species, billions of spawn, trillions of creatures — the numbers were off. Besides, half that American audience probably suffered troubled relations with their mothers. The woman next to me whispered, "What is he trying to do? Bore us out of our interest in Buddhism?"

A generation ago the great Tibetan masters who traveled to America, Dilgo Khyentse and the 16th Karmapa, came to plant the dharma, but America itself did not really interest them. By contrast, our contemporary guru has something to give America but also something to gain: not wealth nor women nor fame but something even more intoxicating. Here was the chance to rewrite the age-old story of Buddhism in contemporary terms.

Crestone is the official residence (except when he is teaching elsewhere, which is usually) of such a modern rinpoche. He is in America because he wants to be, and he wants to make Buddhism at home here, too. He is trying to figure it out, what from age-old Buddhism stays and what in the twenty-first century goes. With no-holds-barred openness and playfulness, too, he is an example of a spiritual teacher à la mode.

It is Mark Twain's *Connecticut Yankee in King Arthur's Court*, only in reverse. Tsoknyi Rinpoche III, reared in a monastery practically out of the Middle Ages, suddenly gets dropped into frenzied, futuristic America, knowing nothing about Americans and yet instantly having to plunge into teaching them. Something interesting was bound to happen.

⌒

It is now twenty-five years later, and for Tsoknyi every occasion, even a frivolous one like, say, a party, is an occasion to teach.

In fact, I first met Tsoknyi Rinpoche at a party held at Mark Elliott's house. Crestone would seem an improbable residence for a professional filmmaker, and in my wishy-washy way I once asked Mark about it.

Me: Mark, did moving to Crestone have, uh, well, any effect on, you know, your career?

Mark: Do you mean was it professional suicide? Yes.

Not quite suicide, for we were gathered that night in his editing studio to view his current film in progress. Though eager to see the film, I was more curious to view a rinpoche viewing it.

The film's subject matter was intriguing — the 17th Karmapa, who is only in his twenties but is considered the successor or unifying figure for Tibetan Buddhism, when the Dalai Lama is no longer with us. The producer who commissioned the film had proved treacherous, all charm on the surface, all deceit underneath. He would lie to Mark, blithely break his promises, and issue contradictory directives ("Make it traditionally Tibetan. But make it like *Pulp Fiction*."), and then castigate Mark for whichever one he followed. Mark worried that the producer would not even release the film, to avoid reimbursing his expenses. Mark had invited Tsoknyi to get his opinion on the movie's contents, but I suspected Mark wanted more than amateur film criticism. Such as the answer to, How do you handle a situation when the situation is impossible?

Anyway, I was excited. I had donned my finest finery, for I'd be meeting a *rinpoche* — lifetimes of wisdom in a single body! Perhaps I was expecting too much. Tsoknyi Rinpoche did not exude charisma. He did not utter profundities. He did not quote Buddhist scriptures. He did not bless anybody. Short, almost cuddly, with a round face sporting big, round glasses, he might have passed for a graduate student in electrical engineering — except engineering students don't wear Tibetan robes and are rarely so at ease with themselves. If Hollywood ever made a movie about him, someone chiseled and seductive and not resembling Tsoknyi Rinpoche would be cast in the role of Tsoknyi Rinpoche. Yet I was not disappointed, and only later did I realize why.

After the film's showing, everyone showered Mark with compliments. Except for Tsoknyi, who instead got straight to the point. "Will the producer let you make the film you want?" he asked. "Will he let you make the best film you can?"

Mark sighed: "Probably not." Mark confessed that, utterly discouraged, he had thought of throwing in the towel and going on a meditation retreat. Meditation is in Buddhism the cure for whatever ails you. Surely Tsoknyi would approve of Mark's plans to exchange worldly frustrations for Buddhist repose.

But Tsoknyi never once referred to Buddhism; instead he entered into Mark's knot of travail and attempted to untie that knot. Should the situation become unbearable, Tsoknyi said, you may have no choice but to drop it — but only for a little while. If Mark could alternate, in a pas de deux of now-off now-on, he would slip through the producer's grasp and get done what needed to get done.*

Besides, a little ordeal was worth going through to show to the world an inspiring, extraordinary being — to reveal to the world extraordinariness.

The talk in the room now meandered, as it often does at parties, into gossip. A rebel rinpoche in Crestone named Yongzin was reportedly threatening to write a tell-all memoir, to sweep all the dirt about Tibetan Buddhism out from under the carpet. "Did this Yongzin," Tsoknyi asked Mark, "suffer psychological wounds growing up?"

Mark: As a matter of fact, he did.

Tsoknyi: And has he healed them?

Mark: As a matter of fact, he hasn't.

Tsoknyi: Then he has nothing to write about.

Miserable childhoods revisited (Augusten Burroughs, David Sedaris, Jeannette Walls) are the stuff of bestsellers, but bestsellers were not Tsoknyi's domain. "I teach one thing only," the Buddha declared, "the overcoming of suffering." That was evidently what interested Tsoknyi.

---

* Tsoknyi's assessment proved correct. Mark finished the film, called *Bodhisattva*, and despite the producer's objections and interference, the film has been shown around the world.

As mentioned earlier, I had dressed up: black trousers and maroon shirt (just for fun — maroon's the color a Tibetan lama wears). As he was leaving, Tsoknyi stopped, straightened my collar, and suggested: "You should wash your shirts more often." Oh no, I hadn't noticed its subdued carnival of previous spills. "Outside and inside," he said, "reinforce each other." Though his words could have sounded harsh, Tsoknyi immediately changed their tenor by adding, "In Tibet you would be considered a natural yogi."

That night Tsoknyi's actions suggested to me what a contemporary spiritual teacher might be. He or she is not some God-channeling, holy book–interpreting, truth-expounding, morality-upholding minister whom many of us remember from our childhoods. For a contemporary spiritual teacher, psychological acumen may take the place of a theological text, and instead of dogma we have undogmatic attention to the person at hand — as Tsoknyi had attended to Mark. Tsoknyi appeared to place life before religion, for only in that way did it *become* religion.

It had not always been this way. When he first came to this country, a quarter century back, Tsoknyi taught in the traditional manner. At an early retreat of his, a young woman in a tie-dyed dress had poured out her endless troubles to him. She was on the verge of suicide, she wailed, asking what she should do. Tsoknyi told her to look beneath her disturbed emotions, into the basic clear nature of mind. (Probably not very helpful — if she could do that, she wouldn't have needed to be there.) Today Tsoknyi's answer to such a person might be, "Did you take your meds?"

Just as Father Dave has shifted a religious approach from

right creed (orthodoxy) to right experience (orthopraxy), so Tsoknyi has changed the *what* of religion (right and wrong, ethics, eschatology, etc.) into *how* (how to handle problems, how to counter fear and depression, how to psychologically activate our better nature). If the various faiths enlisted enough Father Daves and Tsoknyi Rinpoches, religion might never be the same again.

Interlude: A New Mantra, Followed by Lunch at the Bliss

Should you become interested in contemporary spirituality, first thing, go out and buy a life vest. For you may soon be drowning in a sea of platitudes: "each moment be mindful" or "live in the present" or "be positive, no matter what" (which, even when sound advice, gets worn thin). Tsoknyi had been so refreshing at the party because he expressed things I'd never heard before.

For instance? At one point he announced that he had a new mantra. "What is it, Rinpoche?" people eagerly asked. "What is your new mantra?" Tsoknyi said, "Simply this: *It is real, but it is not true.*" Frankly, I was perplexed. Weren't *real* and *true* interchangeable?

The next day, heading into town to have lunch at the Bliss Café (then the one restaurant/bar/hangout in town), I continued to mull over that real-versus-true difference. I could make a little sense of it. *Real*: every day (when it's not overcast) we can see the sun rise and the sun set; *true*: as the Earth circles the sun, there is neither rising nor setting. Probably all religions rely on this distinction between real (or relative) truth and absolute truth, in order to counter momentary obsessions that at the time seem only too real.

Here is a personal sort-of example.* *In reality*, Washington, DC, is a better place for me to *live*. Arriving back in DC from Crestone, I land in every creature comfort and necessity, in deliciously oxygen-laden air, in more civilized temperatures, in the most politically liberal city in America and architecturally its handsomest. Yet in DC many people might as well wear blinders, so blinkered is their view of what's existentially permissible, and in that constricted atmosphere I wind tighter and the unvoiced part of me grows more silent. *In truth*, Crestone is a better place for me to *be*, for it supports a wider spectrum of what constitutes a legitimate experience, and in that atmosphere I gradually shake free enough to hold less and less of myself back. The better reality versus the better truth: What to do?

Outside the Bliss, lo and behold — a sight I'd never encountered in Crestone before and, just possibly, an illustration of Tsoknyi's real-versus-true distinction. Squatting on the ground was a beggar. He looked the genuine scruffy article, whom in a gritty city you'd walk past without noticing. His Goodwill trousers were ratty and he wore no shirt, revealing the blobby, amorphous fat that comes from a diet of four-day-old doughnuts found in dumpsters. That was the reality; the truth, it turned out, was something else. Although only passing through, he was a Crestone kind of panhandler. John (for

---

* The reason I say *sort-of* is because truth, in the way Tsoknyi means it, cannot be entirely rendered in discursive prose. It cannot be analytically pinpointed, but like certain concepts — *space* is another — it can be wordlessly intuited; it can be experienced.

such was his name) was begging as part of what he called a "dharma tour." All his life the prospect of falling on bad luck and being reduced to begging had terrified him. To confront those fears, he had voluntarily assumed that fate, thus forcing the fears to the fore, where he hoped to leave their threatening reality behind and reach a deeper truth in himself.

Just then Neil Hogan walked up. Neil looks and talks like a good ol' boy from West Virginia — that's the reality — but the truth is that his years working in Africa and practicing Buddhism have made him underneath a fairly sophisticated citizen of the world. Always generous, Neil signaled to the incongruous beggar in Crestone: "Come, let's have lunch. My treat." For a beggar John was quite fussy about how his barbecued yak burger had to be prepared. The reality at that table was that it would be hard to find a more mismatched trio: a West Virginia Buddhist, a voluntary beggar, and me, whatever I am. In truth, though, it wasn't awkward at all but quite comfortable, as mismatched lunch mates sank into a substratum of ease together, like three ex–high school buddies shooting the breeze.

Back to Tsoknyi. Who *was* this man teaching the difference between real and true, which is actually teaching conditioned human beings how, despite their conditioning, they can inhabit the unconditional?* I scavenged for info and gossip from his students in Crestone, and below is what I came up

---

*   See chapter 9.

with, both about his life before America and about how he made the great transition to becoming a religious teacher in the unknown New World.

Before the Chinese conquest, few Tibetans ever speculated what being born outside Tibet would have been like. Probably like falling off the edge of the world. For Tsoknyi to have been born outside Tibet, though, was heavenly good luck. When his father, Tulku Urgyen,* escaped Tibet, it ensured that his sons could practice Buddhism freely, without endangering their lives. In Tibet the Chinese overlords were implementing a policy of "one book = one death," so hardly anyone dared possess a single volume about the dharma. A world away, in rural Nepal, young Tsoknyi was playing carefree in fields and by streams, and everywhere Buddhism was on open affectionate display. In that atmosphere, Tsoknyi became an open and affectionate child.

Ordinarily a rinpoche or conscious reincarnation gets recognized at around age two or three, by age four is studying all day in the monastery, by age six memorizing complete texts, and by age eight going on solitary retreats. Yet not until he was eight was Tulku Urgyen's third son recognized as the reincarnation of Tsoknyi II, who had died in a Chinese gulag, and he did not enter a monastery till he was around age twelve. Thus he possessed something few rinpoches ever had — a normal, happy childhood.

But beginning late, he had a lot of catching up to do, and

---

* Tulku Urgyen, a major force in preserving Tibetan Buddhism, may have been the most modest person ever considered enlightened. He concludes his memoirs: "Personally, I have eaten a lot of meals and slept in between. That's my life story in short."

to add to that pressure, many older lamas at the monastery were constantly reminding him, "No, that's not the way you, as Tsoknyi, do it." The once carefree boy rigidified into a confused, troubled adolescent. Everything he read in the monastery library seemed to condemn him. Bad thoughts create bad karma, the books said. Well, Tsoknyi's thoughts were all bad, about sneaking into town and flirting with girls, so he concluded, *I must be a bad person.* What, then, was he doing in a monastery? Bewildered and tormented, Tsoknyi might have become, he later thought, one more fucked-up monk. (If he did not become a psychological basket case, Tsoknyi added, then there's hope for anybody.)

Possibly the remembrance from childhood that happiness is attainable saved him. Besides, when he felt overwhelmed, he would visit his father, who seemed to understand his perplexities and, wondrously, could dispel them. Tulku Urgyen taught him how to see through troubling thoughts. Learning how his worries and doubts were mentally constructed was the boy's introduction to the advanced teaching of *dzogchen*, to the nature of consciousness itself, for which he would later gain renown for teaching in the West.

When, barely twenty, he was invited to America to teach, Tsoknyi doubted he was up to the challenge. Nervously he asked his father for advice. "Advice?" Tulku Urgyen answered. "When they lavish praise on you in America, say, 'Thank you.' And the next moment forget it." Since he was unlikely to be praised (the opposite was the worry), he could not see the value of such advice. Yet if he was not prepared for America, he was at least curious about it. Tsoknyi arrived here to teach *and* to learn. Instead of feeling himself complete, he was a work in progress. And thus he imported with him not a two-and-a-half-millennia-old religion, but Buddhism itself as a work in progress.

When Tsoknyi arrived in America, he made an astonishing discovery. He had come to a land of sages. Everyone was on his or her way to becoming realized and wise. Americans were masters of logic, they used rational exposition, they had lightning-quick minds. Those who became his students had studied for years on end, reflected endlessly, delved, experimented, sat at the feet of spiritual teachers, and amassed more wisdom than exists in any five books of the Bible. This, he thought, is going to be a piece of cake.

Only gradually did he observe beneath the lucid flow of intelligence the psychological mayhem that often constitutes our emotional lives. Compared to average Tibetans, we are intellectual wizards, but compared to them psychologically we can be a mess, as unstable as if balanced on one foot. How do you work with sensible minds that are linked to screwed-up emotions? Even the basic insights of Buddhism could turn into confusion, if interpreted through a student's neurotic lens. No, not a piece of cake after all.

Tsoknyi rummaged through his tradition to find what idea he could teach to these proud, almost too clever intellects. Finally, he conceded: maybe there wasn't one. The Western spiritual heritage already overflowed with beautiful wisdom accumulated over thousands of years, populated by sages and saviors and savants at every point on its spectrum.

It offered no end-of-life-transforming truths, yet people were still as sunk in foibles, greed, and conflicts as ever. What good could one more beautiful thought do? Besides, spiritual truths are often used to escape from rather than to face one's challenging situations.

If there was nothing Tsoknyi could add to the storied treasure house of wisdom, then just possibly he might subtract. Religion has customarily taken the human animal and added on something: added on God, added on divine destinations, added on golden rules, added on heaven and hell. What would religion's function be if its slate were wiped clean of all that? Tsoknyi subtracts that divine paraphernalia; he subtracts dogma and theology; subtracts even having to believe in anything.

Instead he uses Buddhism to teach how to be a person sound in mind and heart. Gaining implementable knowledge about meditation, compassion, detachment, impermanence, mindfulness, etc. helps a person calm down, and ordinary existence becomes less intractable, more likable. Tsoknyi calls this "happiness Buddhism" or "therapy Buddhism," and, with its helpful techniques for enhancing ordinary life, he has no doubt that its obvious usefulness will help it thrive in the West.

There is, however, if not a problem with then a *grave* limitation to happiness Buddhism, he teaches. For even if daily life could be made into one continuous party, that party is on a houseboat heading blindly toward fatal rapids (sickness, old age, and death). Is there a way, at least in felt experience, to exit that doomed party? At his retreats Tsoknyi says he teaches two things: how to be *a healthy human being* and how to be *beyond human*. Beyond human?* To be at once human and beyond human limitation could serve as the very definition of enlightenment. Enlightenment Buddhism, as Tsoknyi calls it, gets at the dirt, or rather the hurt, overlooked after happiness or therapy Buddhism has cleaned the house.

Here would be the logical place to discuss enlightenment (both Buddhist and nonaffiliated enlightenment). Now, nothing is easier to describe than enlightenment in the abstract — it's to be perfect in compassion, perfect in happiness, perfect in comprehension — but to show how it's actually lived out and how one gets there, that's more difficult and first requires several station stops along the way. Those station stops are the chapters in part 3, where we shall meet Tsoknyi Rinpoche again. Meanwhile, if we spy on how he lives, not in the old Himalayas but in today's U S of A, we will at least get a partial preview.

⪜

Tsoknyi has what most people would covet: gratifying work, recognition, a beautiful spouse, bright children, and faithful friends — and they do make him happy. Yet even so, most of us would hardly covet his way of living.

His personal life does not center on himself. His mind's activities do not center on thoughts. His afterwork and off-hours (if he *has* off-hours) do not center on family and home. Tsoknyi is married to a woman likened to a Tibetan Jacqueline

---

* But what's wrong with "simply" being a human, healthy in body and outlook? This quite sensible question is addressed in chapter 11, at the beginning of the discussion of enlightenment.

Kennedy, and they have two daughters.* But Tsoknyi's real home is the road (or more accurately, the plane): he's always traveling, always teaching elsewhere. Ever to be waving goodbye comes with his job description, but when he leaves on the next teaching trip (and he is always leaving on the next teaching trip), the family is loving and accepting. For most of us days are chopped up and divided by partitions — family on one side and everyone else on the other; or here over here versus there over there; or traveling versus arriving; or work versus pleasure. Perhaps Tsoknyi's most singular achievement was dismantling those partitions.

Earlier Tsoknyi had wanted a home in the old-fashioned sense, a place where he could forget work and unwind in the privacy of his family and perhaps even go on a vacation now and then. Gone are those days; gone are those desires. He no longer wants private or exclusionary pleasures. Beginning at 8:30 AM he starts interacting with people, and as the day

---

* What are the daughters of a rinpoche like, specifically Tsoknyi Rinpoche's? Tsoknyi was the opposite of a strict or authoritarian father, allowing his daughters free rein. He figured that — for example — if they left their room a mess, later when they got older and had boyfriends over, they'd keep it immaculate. And so it proved. When his oldest daughter, Kunchok, (age twenty-five in 2018) entered her teens in Crestone, she behaved like many teenage American girls. Yet today Kunchok is a nun at South India's largest Buddhist monastery, undertaking a rigorous nine-year course to become a *khenpo* (like a PhD in Tibetan Buddhism times ten). The younger daughter, Lhabu-la, (eighteen in 2018) appears made from a different mold. Popular and athletic, she aims to study business economics at a college like Stanford. Yet when she was a little girl, nobody in Crestone had ever seen another child like her. Whatever she had, no matter how much she liked it, she would give it to absolutely anybody who needed or wanted it. Evidently the apples did not fall far from the tree.

unfolds he may meet with dozens of people, each for whom that much-anticipated meeting weighs all-important. From morning to night, one after another, they spill out their dramas and traumas to him. It's a schedule that might well exhaust anyone, and not long ago it was exhausting Tsoknyi.

For his exhaustion he did not blame that chockablock schedule; he blamed himself. His gentle father, Tulku Urgyen, had done five times more. The Dalai Lama does twenty times more. Yet they never seemed tired and they never needed a day off. If those old Buddhists enjoyed such effortless stamina, why couldn't a contemporary model experience the same?

A half dozen years ago, in such a weary state, Tsoknyi found himself in Bodh Gaya, India, sitting under the very bodhi tree beneath which the Buddha became enlightened. Then and there he prayed: he prayed for clarity. Suddenly his teachers came to mind, the great Dilgo Khyentse and the 16th Karmapa, and how at a certain point their personal lives simply fell away, like a snake sloughing off its old skin. Tsoknyi made a vow to emulate their example, to downgrade his personal priorities.

Subsequently, no longer racing around to fulfill the ego's demands for its own gratification ("I want this; I need that"), Tsoknyi now rarely gets tired. Being at peace in himself provides him the rest he needs, and now he does not want even that rest. Whatever comes as a side effect of helping others, let it come. The downgrading of personal requirements may have little to do with the old, otherworldly spirituality of God and heaven, but it may get him to a similar place of beyond-human safety.

When his vision came to him in Bodh Gaya, at that very moment a leaf from the legendary bodhi tree fell off, and among the crowd there, it floated toward him. Others grabbed for it, but Tsoknyi, nearer, deftly grasped it. Surely, he thought, this was a sign, a confirmation of his just-made vow. Tsoknyi strolled away pleased with himself but abruptly stopped. I just took a vow, he realized, to put others first and here I am, snatching this leaf for myself. He nearly laughed: I must be a terrible person.

Postscript — or a Tentative Evaluation

A few people who have attended Tsoknyi's retreats have faulted them for being burdened with too much Tibetan language and exotic ritual, while others object, to the contrary, that he has oversimplified complex, demanding teachings in order to accommodate Western audiences. Those critics suggest that what Tsoknyi is teaching is Buddhism Lite.

But then Father Dave's spirituality, with its reluctance to judge, its receptivity to other faiths, and its unconcern with conversions, may express a newer Christianity — Christianity Lite? Religion has been heavy for so long, weighted not only with intolerance and crusades but also with guilty consciences and repressed desires, that perhaps a good word may be said for Religion Lite?

Indeed, over the past century religion has in many quarters relaxed its once-heavy iron grip. The present pope, Francis, might be considered a "lite" pontiff, who has eased the papacy's two-ton thumbprint of infallibility and harsh dogmatisms. Elsewhere, the mystical wisdom of the East, which once required taking perilous journeys and mastering tongue-twisting languages to fathom, is now available with two clicks on the internet. Twenty-first-century religion, in such instances, appears as at home in the modern world as secularism.

Whatever else it does, Tsoknyi's or Father Dave's lighter religion does not lend itself to warmongering or intolerance or narrowed outlooks. Theirs is a faith that does not set itself above or apart, does not look down on those who believe differently. Rather, it regards them tenderheartedly, as secret sharers of the same suffering and blessed condition.

On the mountainside above Crestone, Tsoknyi Rinpoche teaches not *what*, not God and moral law, but *how*: how to personally ripen and realize your inherently enlightened nature. That realization requires no credos, no deity, no otherworldly apparatus. How can that be called religion? Yet with its goal of transcending egotistic limitations, and its vision of "beyond human," how could it not be? Every religion culminates, finally, in a vision beyond the ordinary and the mundane: it's what makes it a religion. Tsoknyi's and Father Dave's *beyond* transpires not in a heavenly addendum but in the here and now, even in earthy little Crestone.

4. More Religions Than One

A fundamentalist's fantasy: they of the true faith are practicing their religion much as God whispered it into the ear of Moses or Jesus or Muhammad. But such a vision obscures how — in our dizzying, everything-changing world — religions, too, in their outward forms and inward meanings, are continually in upheaval. Indeed, at times it seems that only two of the old pillars, or truisms, of religion are left standing. The question here is, Do even those two remain true, or standing, in Crestone?

The first truism: Ultimately, for it to be effective, you can practice only one religion in depth. By all means, explore other faiths, appropriate whatever is of worth in them, but then integrate it into your birth or home religion. A physician does not specialize in oncology *and* radiology *and* psychiatry *and* gynecology, because then he or she would likely never master the complexities of any one of them. Likewise for religious practice. In this chapter a Taoist sage admonishes: To reach water buried deep underground, you do not dig eight wells, each ten feet shallow, but one well eighty feet deep.

The second truism of the religious life: You do need to

practice some organized or traditional faith. It's all well and good to say, "I am spiritual but not religious" and to assemble from different wisdom traditions and self-help guides a true-to-you spirituality. But if your world collapses around you, you may have nothing larger than yourself — no institution, no community, no hard practices you neglected — to see you through the bad times, which is when a traditional religion can be most helpful.

These two observations used to be reckoned plain common sense. In this chapter we meet a couple of Crestonians who have become more accomplished and capable individuals by practicing several religions, thus challenging the first truism of *one person one faith*. The following chapter, in which equally realized folks follow no religion at all — saints without denomination — challenges the second truism about *religion as necessity*. These successfully multireligious and those luminous nonpractitioners: Are they brothers and sisters under the skin, heralding a new way of being spiritual in the contemporary world?

A Multireligious Mayor Helps a Sick Teenager

To witness multireligiousness in action, let's go straight to the top, to the mayor's office. Except the mayor of Crestone has no office. Better than any stuffy office is the street, where he surprises tourists with, "Hi, I'm Ralph Abrams, the mayor. Welcome to Crestone!" (That announcement of high office worked less well in a Denver strip club, where the girls getting off the poles were unimpressed.) What the Rotary and

Lions Clubs are to other small-town mayors, shamanism, Jungianism, and Tibetan Buddhism are to Ralph.

Small-town mayors are rarely visionaries, but Ralph did have a vision. In this county (Saguache) an average person cannot afford the cost of the average house in Crestone, and he wanted to focus on how ordinary working people — and not only Boulder's wealthy overflow — could live here. He did not lack ideas,* but in small towns any idea often sparks opposition, and small disagreements harden into large ones. Ralph's MO for dealing with these brouhahas? At times he relied on a spiritual approach instead of trading favors or making deals. The Buddhist insight that things are not fixed but the temporary coalescing of disparate factors that would soon disperse helped him accept people and positions he might otherwise have found quarrel with. Likewise, a shamanic sense of subterranean interconnection kept him from partitioning issues into good and bad, allies and enemies.†

Ralph could approach local politics with this flexibility because, while his Jungian side emphasizes developing the

---

* See his plan for Crestone acquiring its own telecommunications network in chapter 9.

† An example would be the financing and building of the handsome new charter school that changed Crestone, for some, from a place where you might not want your children to be educated to a place where you would. On such an important issue around twenty different positions or factions arose: a lot of *us* versus *them* versus *them*. Another small-town politico might have staked out the most sensible position (to her), gathered her allies (sidelining the others), in order to get something done. Ralph did not take a strong position on the charter school, though, but suspended his point of view even as he suspended his ego. Thus he could meet with everyone, with no *me* versus *them*, no friend and no foe. By downplaying his ego and with it his viewpoint, free-ranging creativity and even humor seeped into the situation and the chance of a fray lessened.

self (in Jungian terms, individuating), his Buddhism encourages letting go of that very thing. Anyone in Crestone might well need to do both — alternately fortifying the ego and letting it go; outwardly resisting and inwardly surrendering — in order to live in a harsh, demanding place where things rarely go entirely your way. Ralph's political side furthered his sense of being (in Jungian terms) somebody, which gave him the confidence to become (in Buddhist terms) nobody.

In his political life, being simultaneously Jewish,* Buddhist, shamanic, and Jungian gave Ralph more flexibility to meet situations in Crestone still in flux.

It did in his personal life as well. Ralph once got a phone call from San Diego that his stepdaughter Christina, having suffered a schizophrenic breakdown, was living on the streets. When he talked to Christina, she reported that they — *they!* — had planted computer chips in her brain to monitor her. Another parent might have reckoned schizophrenia beyond his competence and dialed 911. Instead Ralph mentally circled the situation, calling in his assemblage of spiritualities. From a Jungian viewpoint, Ralph recognized that a welling-up of unconscious archetypes was overwhelming his stepdaughter's unstable ego. Christina was lost in delusions, but from the Buddhist viewpoint, most people's realities are chunks flaking off a collective illusion. If they were in the Amazon he could have contracted a shaman to exorcise her "demons." And underlying all was his (latent) Judaism, which encouraged

---

* Sort of Jewish. One year, since his last name is Abrams, I asked if he planned on observing Yom Kippur. "Definitely!" he responded. "I have a date with a Jewish girl."

him to take family responsibility and to suspect that not only family but also community needed to be brought into play.

Such speculations fostered in Ralph the breadth of vision to approach the situation other than by consigning his stepdaughter to a mental hospital. It wasn't the Amazon, and it wouldn't be Jung's clinic in Zurich, he mused, but why not bring Christina to Crestone? Here in the tiny town she could wander about safely instead of being confined to a locked-ward regimen of pills and TV and art therapy. On Christina's first night in Crestone, Ralph brought her to a birthday party for a ninety-one-year-old man, where she told her birthday host about the chips in her head. "Girl, you too?" he exclaimed. "They pulled the same stunt on my brain." Christina's anxiety gradually subsided in Crestone, free of the stigma of being branded *whacko*.

Christina was the beneficiary of Ralph's - - indeed, of Crestone's — redefining religion away from a single-faith dogma into, as Ralph once said, a multispiritual "what works." ("Whatever works" may sound crudely pragmatic, but then one hardly wants a religion that in crises doesn't work.)

A Nature Guide to the Various Worlds

Someone else in Crestone may demonstrate even more clearly what practicing several religions in conjunction can do. John Milton has studied with more masters from more different traditions than quite possibly anybody else in history. His multiple religious perspectives have given him the leeway to work equally well in the White House and with endangered rhinoceroses in Nepal. John hails from that vanishing breed of rugged individuals, often named John — John Muir and Johnny Appleseed and John Burroughs — who forged their identities in the wild. When I first met him, he appeared a handsome, vigorous man in his fifties. But he was surely older, since he'd been undertaking vision quests in the wilderness for more than six decades.

By profession he is a nature guide, but a rather atypical one, one who borrows insights from various faiths to show greenhorns how to live in the wild and return ready to shape a better society. He demonstrates how the different religions can help you, whether you are facing a growling bear or lying in a hospital bed helpless.

About the latter: long flights, with their cramped seating and bad air, can be hard on older passengers. On such a flight a couple of years ago John, though fit and sturdy, suffered an apparent stroke. When he finally reached a hospital, the doctors told him that bed would likely be his new permanent home. The TV in the shared room blared constantly, competing with the screams of the other patients. To cope with this hospital purgatory, John turned to his repertoire of spiritual practices. In one he simply observed concerns and worries as they rose up and fell away. His agitation subsided as he sided with, as it were, the nature of pure awareness rather than what it happened to be momentarily aware of. In this Buddhist practice, he mentally and emotionally took on the other patients' sufferings and in exchange sent them, in waves of empathy, the light calm he was now feeling. Doing so seemed to lessen his pain for entire hours until it was all but forgotten.

What helped most, though, was doing Taoist "internal"

tai chi and qigong, through which John directed his energy into the reestablishment of nerve system patterns. That such self-healing could do what standard Western medicine could not certainly sounds far-fetched, and the hospital doctors could scarcely believe the extent to and the rapidity with which he recovered. When I saw him some months later, except for a semiparalyzed left arm, John was in fine form. By then he was trekking through the woods, leaping on rocks across streams, and climbing the fourteen-thousand-foot peaks in Crestone. The next year he circumambulated Mount Kailash, Tibet's holy mountain — not your typical poststroke activity.

And imagine, Buddhism and Taoism were but two of the items in his armory. John's atypical self-recovery in the hospital made me curious about what he's like when he's at large in the world. And I was curious, too, about what had brought him to Crestone years ago, before the religious groups discovered it, when only some few score miners' descendants lived here.

At age seven, John ventured out (without even knowing the term) on his first vision quest. He spent four days and nights outdoors, feeling wild and kin with everything under the sun and the moon. The woods were what church should be like, the boy thought, not that stuffy building where Sundays died of dullness. At age fourteen John braved his first month alone in the wilderness. In college he supported himself washing dishes and waiting tables, hoarding money for the summers, when he would trespass where no white man had dared go before. In Canada's Northwest Territories he scaled the highest previously unclimbed peak in the Rockies. After graduation, John says, he got lucky.

Hired to manage the Conservation Foundation's international division, for the next dozen years he traveled the world over. The term *conservation* had begun to sound dated, as though instead of living in harmony with nature man was conserving, once more controlling it. John organized two conferences on *ecology* (the new buzzword), which led to federal government projects being reviewed for their *environmental* impact. He was then named the first environmental advisor to the Council of Economic Advisors (working in the White House under the Nixon administration).

"First-world" countries then considered themselves great humanitarian civilizations, with their superior technological know-how rescuing the wretched backward of the Earth. The United States, for example, planned to erect in Vietnam one hundred and fifty state-of-the-art dams along the Mekong River and its tributaries, and John was invited to do the environmental impact study. His study showed sheer catastrophe being wreaked: damming the river would uproot people of the Delta and transfer them to areas where their skills would be useless. Also, schistosomiasis, kept under control by the seasonal drying out of the area, would, with the dams' standing lakes, leap to epidemic proportions (from 10 percent to an estimated 90 percent of the population being affected). John's studies sent a shock wave through the development-aid world, knocking the halo off first-world techno-saints saving the "third world" from its own pathetic helplessness.

Even while he was fighting the good ecological fight, though, something else was on his mind. Earlier, in college, when everyone else was at football games, John would be meditating, at a time when meditation in this country was barely heard of. When later John was hired to save the endangered rhinoceroses of Nepal,* in his time off he would seek out obscure spiritual teachers, to initiate him in a little-known knowledge as endangered as those rhinoceroses. The great lamas who had been practically gods in Tibet now possessed in exile no other luxury than time and would happily converse with the few Westerners like John who sought them out. Elsewhere in Asia John located the last surviving adepts of Taoism, who instructed him in ancient methods for bringing into harmonious alignment bodily processes. He found as well a Hindu sadhu to teach him left-handed tantra or secret yogic techniques practically unheard of by Westerners then.

Once back in America John speculated: What if he dared join the two sides of himself, the naturalist and the seeker? Could the mind-body techniques he learned in Asia supplement the wilderness skills he had been honing since boyhood? If so, he would have in his quiver more arrows, or possibilities, than most nature guides. He began scouting for some untamed place where he could effect this marriage of wilderness experience and spiritual traditions. The remote place John finally found was the San Luis Valley, the Sangre de Cristos, and Crestone.

---

* When John began, fewer than fifty rhinoceroses were left in Nepal, and after his work there were more than a thousand.

John moved into a rickety one-room cabin when Crestone boasted a grand total population of 100* and he bought land (which is dirt) when it was dirt-cheap here, and he christened it the Sacred Land Trust. On the Sacred Land Trust John would lead retreats for people to reconnect inner and outer as a way of resacramentalizing both their surroundings and themselves. (Elsewhere he has conducted thousands of similar nature retreats around the world.)

The great religions are replete with tools, John finds, for ennobling the nature inside ourselves as well as the nature outside. By selectively combining four religions, John has shown his students how to do what they never thought they could — like survive in the wilderness without shelter or, temporarily, food. An invisible Buddhist, Taoist, Hindu Tantrist, and Native American shaman are silently whispering in his ear as he coaches his nature retreatants both on how to relate to the wild and on how to transform themselves in it.

In Nepal John had succeeded in locating a humble or "hidden" tantric guru. This guru, Vadsu Dev, made a prophecy that for once, to John's relief, did not come true. Vadsu Dev's principal teaching (utterly simple, though it sounds utterly impossible) was to completely surrender yourself to whatever

---

*   That was Crestone's population then. And today? Roughly 1,500 in summer and 750 the rest of the year.

happens. John's version of surrender, Vadsu Dev said, would involve being bitten by a cobra and then transmuting its deadly poison without external antidote. That prophecy caused John no little anxiety, until he finally left Nepal, relieved not to have stepped blindly on an outraged cobra.

A few years later John was at his annual retreat in Baja California. The pelicans paraded up and down the beach, comical and stately, the lords and ladies of a portentous waddling society. As he was returning from the beach to the campsite, John was asked by a student, "What is tantra?" He was about to answer ("the thread running through and connecting us and the universe") when time stood still. John had been bitten by one fang of a rattlesnake. He walked carefully back to his cabin, so as not to alarm the woman. His lower leg was becoming paralyzed, however, and if the venom reached his heart he would die. Fortunately, a mile away, in Todos Santos, was a health clinic — so from his cabin he headed in that direction.

As he inched his way along, John had a mental image of Vadsu Dev and in his mind heard him say, "Now. It is time now." John reversed direction from the clinic and returned to his cabin. The toxin of a rattlesnake affects its victim neurologically. Wherever John looked he felt a sense of kinship with it, and euphoria pervaded, it seemed, every atom of his being. Then, as though a switch had been flipped, the bliss succumbed to an inexplicable rage welling up in him. In his weakened physical and unstable mental condition, he required an attendant constantly, and pity the attendant, for John's alternations between animosity, pride, and sullen fury hardly made him congenial company.

Snakes and snake venom have played a crucial role in healing throughout the shamanic world,* especially if the trouble addressed is partly physical and partly spiritual. Vadsu Dev evidently recognized that certain snake venom could work almost like a drug to effect in John the necessary transformation. And so it proved: John's alternations between euphoria and sullen fury in a body too feeble to resist either continued for the next six months, but at the end of it all his inner turmoil subsided, leaving him healthier and emotionally clearer than he had ever felt before. Now if those negative states John experienced during that ordeal (and other times, too) ever return, they are transparent, like a bad TV program he knows how to turn off.

In his dark night of the soul John appropriated Vadsu Dev's unconditional acceptance as he willingly submitted to the effects of the venom, at times not knowing whether he would recover. *Accept* because reality, he learned during his ordeal, is beyond what we know or can know. (Reality is stranger than fiction: Who would have guessed that a snakebite could do what it did for John?) Now when he sends his students on vision quests, he tells them that presence and submission are as necessary as knife or compass. With such acceptance, some of his students have endured days in the wilderness without shelter or food.

Which leads to a question: Why would anyone want to do that?

---

*   See, for example, Tété-Michel Kpomassie's *An African in Greenland*.

Here's the curriculum. To acclimatize us pampered city folk, John first sends us on Nature Quests, where we spend three days and nights in the wild. Then over time some progress to Sacred Passages, where they might spend anywhere from twenty-eight to forty-four days in the mountains above Crestone, all by their lonesome. Only then (and only occasionally) — at the far end of the spectrum of extreme experience — comes the Vision Quest.

Patterned after Native American retreats, Vision Quests leave you in the wilderness with only — actually, there's no *with*. You bring no tent to protect you from the elements. Like Adam or Eve, you wear no clothes. You eat no food. Scarcely any water do you drink. And this is like child's play compared to the last trial: as the moon replaces the sun, you will not sleep under it; no retreating into dreams as day to night succumbs. The purpose of these "five sacrifices" — four days with no food, no shelter, no clothing, little water, no sleep — is to shake and wake you from the slumber of unconscious, automatic habits, what you do without even realizing you are doing it.

In the previous chapter we heard Tsoknyi Rinpoche speak of the importance of going beyond human. A vision quest could be described as a journey to the beyond human but detouring through daunting human ordeals to get there. To prepare you, John does not teach you how to set up a campsite or what to do in case of snakebite. Rather, he extracts from the various spiritual traditions insights and practices that will see you through on a different level. Thus prepared, when it is rainy and cold (remember, the Sangre de Cristos above

Crestone rise up to fourteen thousand feet), and you are bereft of food and sleep, you just may make it through.

Although we might not willingly undergo a Vision Quest ourselves, we can vicariously follow one of John's students into the seemingly impossible. Let us shadow him to see what this adventure into the human-beyond-human reaps.

This particular student of John's is not one but all of the following: an engineer, an economist, a systems operations analyst, a mathematician, a founder of complexity theory, an expert in population studies, and the youngest person ever to hold an endowed chair at Stanford University. Hanne Strong likes prominent people and invited this Brian Arthur to visit Crestone but then forgot about it and was away when he arrived.

Poking about this town — if you can even call it a town, thought Brian — he chanced upon John Milton. Brian: "What do you do, Mr. Milton?" John: "Me? I send people out into nature in a sacred way." Really? Sometimes Brian had daydreamed of such a possibility, of entering the natural world in a state of heightened response. A fleeting fantasy, nonsense — but here, in this place that was no place, had that nonsense suddenly turned into opportunity?

At Stanford some years earlier, Brian read that a Taoist teacher was lecturing at 6:30 AM in San Francisco, and his curiosity pricked him enough to be there at that ungodly hour. Only six hours later the sage (by name Kwong ke chin) appeared, and talked, and talked, late into the night, after which he invited anyone interested to join him at 1:30 AM at a restaurant in Chinatown. Brian had an intuition he would sit next to the Taoist teacher at dinner, so he prepared his question in advance: *What's in it for me, if I get involved in your Taoism?* "Ah," Kwong ke chin replied, "you may live a quarter century longer. You may do an extra quarter century of productive research. You will become a good professor." And with no further ado he abruptly ignored Brian and conversed with the person on his other side. After a few minutes the teacher turned back to Brian, and added, "If that's all you want..."

Evidently it was not all Brian wanted. He began flying regularly to Hong Kong to study with Kwong, who after some years invited Brian to become his spiritual successor. In the annals of Taoism such an invitation to a *gweilo* (pale ghost or Caucasian) was without precedent. But Brian longed to continue his scientific work and thus was in a real quandary when he arrived on his visit to Crestone.

Imagine, then, Brian's amazement when John began to mention the many Taoist masters he had studied with, and that Taoism was in fact a door through which his students entered nature. On a whim Brian had come to Crestone — a whim that would lead him into a two-decade relationship with John and more than forty Sacred Passages in nature, which sometimes he finds easy, sometimes hard, but he knew enough not to attempt that hardest of all, a Vision Quest.

In 1995 Brian was doing a twenty-eight-day Sacred Passage above Crestone, and for a change it was going unusually well. Until, that is, John came to check on him and nonchalantly said, "Oh, by the way, a Vision Quest should be part of what you're doing." *No food, no clothing, no sleep? Uh-uh.*

Brian thought, *I'll let John waste his breath trying to persuade me.* But John just walked away. Torn, agitated, Brian called after him, "What do I do if I'm naked and have no shelter and a bear comes growling at me?" John glanced over his shoulder and said, "Pray."

Brian keeps a John Milton index. The index measures how many times, during a retreat, he curses John.

Four days sans food, sans clothes, sans sleep in the shelterless night: Brian knew for a certainty he couldn't do it. He closed his eyes and had a fleeting image of a Las Vegas slot machine hitting jackpot and gold coins raining down. He took that for a...maybe he should try.

Okay, he would try to try. Brian wandered off from his campsite and drew an eight-foot circle demarcating the boundaries of the Vision Quest. Obviously he did not have to bring along much. The only thing you need on a Vision Quest is courage, and in lieu of that Brian took a small jar of honey in a plastic bag to ward off hypothermia (sugar boosts the body's energy). It did freeze the first night, numbing him almost beyond consciousness, but when morning came the sun's penetrating rays warmed his icicle-like body. All too soon, though, the well-being he was experiencing got interrupted by an intruder stomping through the foliage. Oh, but it wasn't a mountain climber. It was a bear, attracted by the smell of honey. With all the force he could muster Brian hurled the jar of honey, aiming it at the stream. He could have fled the demarcated circle but was unexpectedly reluctant to terminate his Vision Quest. Instead Brian meditated, and though the bear did not immediately go away, his fear of it did.

The hardest part for Brian was not sleeping. The first nights, when dead-tired, his antidote for eyes closing dreamward was to support himself by leaning on a stick. If he fell asleep for a second, plop went the stick and crashed him into wakefulness. By the third night he no longer needed the stick; by then Brian felt such energy coursing through him he could not have slept had he wanted to. His heightened sensitivity registered unfamiliar perceptions outside the usual range of consciousness. The tinkling stream nearby, for example, he heard as chords of music. He realized that lack of food and sleep might well be playing tricks with his mental functioning. But if these enchanted sensations were hallucinations, he accepted them as sacred hallucinations from a different key of nature.

After so many Sacred Passages and now his Vision Quest, Brian emerged with a different sense of himself. What had allowed him, he wondered, to go for days without food or sleep, to discount his fears, and to see in the landscape a reflection of his inner self? He certainly had no Daniel Boone– or Jim Bridger–like mastery of wilderness skills, which anyway would have produced a different experience. It must have been John's borrowings from different religions subtly transmitted to him that had allowed seemingly impossible ordeals in the wild to become possible. Would it not be strange if, on a Colorado mountainside deep in the American West, at play was:

- a Taoist-like regulation of inner energy (so his impulses could be controlled instead of their controlling him),

- a Buddhist transparency of thoughts (so he recognized his dread of bears, say, as a panicky feeling and not a truth about bears),

- a Hindu intertwined kinship of self and world (so on one side he did not face a hostile or indifferent wilderness on the other), and

- the shamanic conduit between our visible world and evanescent otherworlds (which allies the human spirit with other spirits or energies in nature).

John's was its own complex system, Brian realized, that conjoined different religious insights to reinforce one another — and him. Returning to Stanford, Brian resigned his endowed chair and moved to Santa Fe to help found an institute for the study of complexity theory.

At first Brian had looked askance at how John borrowed from this religion and that, picking and choosing, it seemed to Brian, at whim. Brian's old Taoist master Kwong ke chin had warned against such spiritual collages. "Should you want to tap water buried deep underground," Kwong had cautioned, "you don't dig eight ten-foot wells. You dig one well eighty feet deep." Remembering that warning, Brian confronted John.

Brian: "Don't you think, John, it's better to go into one religion deeply?"

John: "No, it's better to go into four religions deeply."

Brian: "Now, why would that be?"

John: "Each religion comes with unnecessary baggage. If you know only one religion, you may mistake its cultural expression for the quite useful knowledge it teaches. Know several, and the superfluous in each falls away, leaving the saving essence — which, when you face unknown fears, may save you."

And what would those religions' underlying truths look like, stripped of their historical and cultural accretions? Here are a couple of John's experiences and realizations, divested of any denominational label.

First: *Immanence and transcendence, Earth and heaven, are not two separate realities but flow in a single stream.*

The major event in John's life took place — how prosaic — in an ordinary bed-and-breakfast. The year was 1984 (as in Orwell's novel) and the place was Wurtsboro, New York, where years before his father had died in a canoeing accident.

That particular night John had returned to the B&B barely in the nick of time, before the dark glowering heavens unleashed a truly epic downpour. As John lay in bed, a deafening thunderbolt shook the room, as though Earth itself were being torn asunder. A jolt, a spasm, convulsed his body — it felt like lightning shooting through him — but if that were so he would probably be dead. So possibly a close miss.

As in a near-death experience, John felt whirled down a dark tunnel into an unearthly light, into seemingly conscious luminousness. This light/awareness felt more ecstatic than a dozen orgasms, and for six hours (a near-death experience lasts but minutes) he lived through what seemed lifetimes of ecstatic sensations and wordless realizations. When they finally subsided, Venus, the morning star, was just appearing in the heavens.

No one can understand him, John says, without understanding what happened that night, and even he cannot explain it. When he tries to convert that ineffable union of being-bliss-clarity into words, he worries it sounds like gibberish. (In an ecstatic trance St. Thomas Aquinas scribbled a beatific vision in crazed indecipherable marks but said that next to it his *Summa Theologica* was but straw.) During those six hours John felt his being rewired, as it were, attuned to a wider range of frequencies.

Most religious traditions posit levels of reality: there is the hierarchy of Earth below and heaven above, immanence and transcendence, relative facts and absolute truth, etc. For John now they collapsed into a single stream of display, of possibility. He hardly knew what to make of his silent, transforming vision, at the B&B, of existence pervaded by consciousness. It reminded him of how in Taoism all things arise out of the same original "Oneness" (a Taoist version of the big bang), and he recalled, too, Tibetan metaphysics, in which matter is ultimately solidified energy or light (a Buddhist $e = mc^2$). After his rewiring that night John felt adaptable and confident enough to work almost anywhere under nearly any condition: for every problem, he sensed, secretly also carried the code to its solution, the way in his vision phenomena had unfolded like a telltale message.

Second experience/realization: *Walmart is a good place to obtain the raw ingredients for a mystical experience.*

John tries to inculcate in his students a receptivity to the possibility of other possibilities — to the surprise of things happening other than expected. He employs unusual methods for achieving that *eureka*. One year he gathered his students on retreat above Crestone and drove them to the nearest sizable town that boasted that site of popular pilgrimage, Walmart. There he had them purchase cheap clocks and instructed them, once back at their various solitary campsites, to gaze steadily at the second hand for two-hour stretches at a time.

Brian Arthur hated the assignment: to be in the middle of the woods staring at a stupid, tick-tick-ticking, made-in-China wall clock was his idea of a not-so-sacred passage to mortal monotony. After a while, though, concentrating on the clock hands sharpened his senses and made his mind extraordinarily present. Then something peculiar happened: the second hand would stop and after a brief spell click back into motion. *Something wrong with the damned clock*, Brian thought, but when he checked it against the reliable watch in his backpack, both told precisely the same minute and hour. What the hell was going on? Well, one's subjective experience of time — whether it's fleeting or dragging — does not necessarily accord with the standard, objective measurements of it. The solid way we perceive things, Brian speculated, may not be the reliable final reality after all. Thanks to that Walmart piece of junk, Brian gained a measure of independence from the reified impersonal dictates that govern most lives, including his, up to then.

At times John seems as ordinary as his name, plain John who likes high-tech gadgets, good coffee, and movies, but at other times, anything but. Or so it seemed to Brian Arthur one day in Walmart when he watched the expression on John's face change, as though John had recognized a long-unseen friend. But nobody was in sight, except far down the aisle a dejected, defeated old man. John strode straight up to him and struck up a conversation.

John: "Sir, I wonder if you can help me?"

Dejected man: "I — I'd be glad to. But there's no way I can help you. Or anybody."

John: "You see, I just returned to my cabin after months away, and it's overrun with mice, mice everywhere. Do you have any idea how I can get rid of them?"

Dejected man (now less dejected): "I was — I am — an exterminator." He produced from his billfold a weathered, crumbled business card apparently from decades ago. A smile, awkward and unpracticed, tried to take shape on his face. "Yes, yes — I can help you!"

Not having been there, I have no idea what John observed that made him surmise the old man was an exterminator (perhaps his clothes?). But how kind and considerate was his approach to him. Kindness and perception and connection — not morals and metaphysics and miracles — that's perhaps a newer idea of the holy. Possibly four religions were needed to refine John's intuition to such a point of empathy and attunement.

The more religions then the merrier? John Milton and Ralph Abrams, innovative and accomplished and usually in fine fettle, might make it seem so. What, though, if some others in Crestone achieved the same result without bothering with religion at all? Then that might require a second glance — a look behind or beyond the scenes of faith — to discover an equivalent heightened felicity, a larger awareness, that you need not be religious to avail yourself of.

And so (in the next chapter) into fewer religions than one — into the less the merrier — we go.

5. Fewer Than One

I

C ould the ultimate religion be — no religion at all? That possibility shocked the progressive Christian audience at Chicago's World Parliament of Religions in 1893. The charismatic Swami Vivekananda delighted them by declaring, "It is wonderful to be born into a religion." Vivekananda then added, "But it is terrible to die in one." It was a slap in the face to their deepest beliefs. Yet two and a half millennia earlier the Buddha had, in a similar vein, compared spiritual teachings to a raft transporting you to the other shore. But once there, the Buddha said, if you still carry the raft (religion), you'll stagger under a needlessly heavy burden.

In Crestone the last (or possibly first?) word on this subject may be that of a modest old potter. Religions are a first step, a necessary first step, Bertha Gotterup says: "Just as having a mother and father is a first step. Eventually, though, we must leave that childhood nest behind."

Old-timers in Crestone believe that, while nobody here

is enlightened, the person who may come closest is Bertha.*
Should you then inquire who, if anybody, might be considered the town's guardian spirit, many would point to Mark
Jacobi. Mark, a stocky white guy with gray dreadlocks, roves
downtown, talking with everyone, making sure everyone's
all right, even schoolkids who with adults other than Mark
only grunt in monosyllables. But neither Mark nor Bertha follows a religious or spiritual tradition. Picture all Crestone's
spiritual practitioners and devotees and seekers in one field.
Then imagine Mark *off to the side* of it, having a much better
time. And Bertha stands at a distance beyond both fields, in
what possibly comes *after* religion.

Crestone boasts ten Buddhist groups, whose practitioners
Mark sometimes asks, "What should you say if asked if you're
a Buddhist?" Comic pause, then, "I'm not attached to it."
Buddhists are supposed to be detached, but religion is what
Mark is not attached to. Here's his idea for the perfect jihad:
the Haidakhandi Ashram challenges the Carmelites to a vol-
leyball tournament, and whoever loses converts. When a fundamentalist rebuked Mark for irreverence, Mark asked him,
"Are you a Christian?" The fundamentalist: "Certainly. And
proud to be." Mark: "Then it is your job to forgive me." Neither Mark nor Bertha is antireligious; they just find much of
organized religion ever so slightly comical.

Yet religion's sense of a life larger than life is practically
the air one breathes in Crestone. It's in the silent mountain grandeur; with all the temples and stupas it's the background even to all the kibitzing around. A spokeswoman for

---

* See "A Note on Dates."

Native American causes, Lorain Fox Davis, described how people change when they move here. They tend to become self-reliant simply to survive in such a harsh and isolated environment. But also, she says, in a remote place without city conveniences they cannot make it alone and become, perhaps for the first time, part of a community, too. And spared many contemporary hassles — no long commutes, no crime, no hurrying crowdedness, no cacophony of noises — they peer ever farther out of their turtle shells. Last, Lorain pointed out, almost everyone here comes to feel a deep connection to the land.

A sense of connection between one's inner and outer landscape? Self-reliance? The good of the community? The softening of the heart? Aren't these some of the values that religion, at its noblest, attempts to inculcate in the individual practitioner? Yet here they are techniques for survival, if you intend to stay and make a go of it. In Crestone some folks thus come close to having a sacred outlook without benefit of clergy.

Unlike many of the best and brightest hereabouts, Mark Jacobi did not come to Crestone for its religion(s). In fact, he has never done anything for religion, except stop attending his parents' church as early as possible, then ignore his father's suggestion to try other denominations, and as for the rest he stayed out of harm's, and churchdom's, way. Yet he is not an unethical man; quite the contrary. Kizzen Laki, editor of the *Crestone Eagle*, observes, "When the emperor is wearing no clothes, Mark is the one who sees it. He has a grade-A bull-shit detector." And she adds, "He does for our town what a church is supposed to, helps make it a community."

How did he become that man religions are designed to give birth to, without any assistance from them?

Mark's story. If Hollywood created an apple-pie all-American town, anchored by a white church with steeple, it might name that town, oh, maybe, Appleton. In 1953 Mark Jacobi was born in Appleton, Wisconsin. He veered off track early, though, by working backstage at the local theatrical company (his older sister was dating the director). Saturday night was like a big toy box where out of nothing, from a few sticks and props, magical worlds of wonder were created. After such a Saturday night, the last thing he wanted early next morning — ugh — was church and Sunday school, a place where no wizardry at all was worked.

About the time Mark turned twenty his father died, and his mother took solace in every right-wing Republican cause. Mark, living at home, received the brunt of her unhappiness and hostility. Then his girlfriend left him. Then he fell off the house roof on which he was working. Today the sixty-year-old Mark would say to that floundering twenty-year-old unsure of himself, "Yes, your father died. And you will die, too. And the way to honor him is by living well now."

Living well? At college a hit of acid was cheaper than going to the movies. *Do the math*, he thought, and having done the math, and the LSD, Mark dropped out of college. He worked variously as a cabdriver, a security guard, and a carpenter, until — doing the math again — he calculated how from Appleton the Big Apple was not even a thousand miles, hardly more than a day away. Wild times ensued. At a trendy New York cross-dressers' bar, a band member cautioned a woman there, "Every man in this city is either gay, married, or severely neurotic." The woman decided, sensibly, to ask the handsomest man there whether that was true. "How would I know?" Mark answered. *If he is secure enough to be in a cross-dressers' bar*, she thought, *he's probably all right.* Thirty years later that woman, Chris Canaly, now his wife, has not reversed that verdict.

Just as he once had found in the local theater group the anti-Appleton, so driving across country Mark chanced upon, in effect, non-America — outside Santa Fe, in a landscape full of pagodas, stupas, and temples. Back in New York, Mark described to his boss that southwestern otherworld. Oh, if you like that sort of crap, his boss said, you should check out this town Crestone in Colorado: it's off the map. *I'm due for my midlife crisis*, Mark thought, *so why not?* Months later, his first sight in Crestone was deer eating apples off the trees. This image of natural harmony was enough for him. As Ralph Abrams would do later, he went straight to the real estate office, and then called Chris and asked, Did she have any suitcases, and did she want to pack them?

Before reaching Crestone, Mark stopped at a hot spring, where he met my old college friend Kenny Dessain. Mark: "What do you have to do in Crestone to survive?" Kenny: "What it never occurred to you to do before." And so it turned out. Mark had done carpentry and construction before (the default job for men in Crestone), but he had never envisioned himself as a crusading civil activist. Over the coming years, however, he would oppose scheme after scheme that would have remade Crestone into a jarring nonversion of its once peaceful self. One after another he fought David-and-Goliath battles that kept a giant New Age pyramid from being built here and that stopped the Air National Guard from night-and-day military testing and that prevented large-scale drilling, which would have dumped the valley's ecosystem into the garbage can. His compatriots in these battles were often motivated by a Christian sense of God's creation or a Buddhist vision of holistic interdependence, but Mark's reasoning was: the Earth was giving him great gifts of, well, everything — food, housing, clothing, beer, medicine — and it was only right to partially return the favor.

Since it was not religion that shaped such a decent man, what has? What are the principles, I wondered, of a good but (in the religious sense) unprincipled man? Instead of asking him directly, I told Mark about a friend from a religious family who decided at age seventeen (as Mark did) that she'd no longer attend church. Surprisingly, her parents consented, but on one condition: she had to come up with seven rules she would live by all her life. The point of telling this story was, slyly, to get Mark to talk about *his* principles, to confess a secret or two about his private code.

Oddly, Mark made no comment about the girl's story. Instead, our talk rambled every which way. Mark talked about Chris's solo retreat under John Milton's guidance. After a few days alone in the wilderness, Mark reported, Chris feared she would go crazy. Then she realized her fears were only her mind tormenting her mind, and her jitters calmed, and amid the trees she danced, naked, for sheer joy.

Only gradually did it dawn on me what Mark was doing. As we talked, just beneath the surface, indirectly and quietly, he was weaving a thread so subtle that at first I did not recognize it for what it was. Camouflaged within his schmoozing about this and that, Mark was slowly coming up with his own seven rules to live by. How unusual to watch before my eyes someone peer into the wordless blur within and from its shadowy recesses discern and delineate his guiding principles. No matter that Mark's seven rules were hardly earth-shattering: to produce them spontaneously on the spot seemed in itself a remarkable feat of self-awareness. Here, then, are the principles of an unprincipled man in Crestone, the beliefs of a nonbeliever.

Rule 1: Do what thou wilt. Let that be the whole of the law. Mark was quoting the occultist and mountebank Aleister Crowley — aka "the Great Beast 666" — who a century ago shocked Victorian morality with his hedonistic libertinism. For Mark "do what thou wilt" is a good rule, though, because frustrated desire is not. Rule 1 takes back responsibility for one's happiness from God, Mommy, and society, leaving it squarely on one's own shoulders. Of course, serial killers, bigots, and ruthless tycoons are doing what they wilt, too — as others about them simply wilt — which is why rule number one needs...

Rule 2: Do no harm. As you do what you want, make sure it's not inflicting on others what they don't want. His first wife (before Chris) did whatever she wanted, which included manipulating, telling blatant lies to and about Mark, and, oh, putting a cigarette out on his face. Mark's rule 2 is never, actually or metaphorically, to put out anything burning on another's psyche or body part.

Rule 3: Religion — you're better off without it. In most traditional religions, if you please God, he/she/they/it will reward you for your display of devout virtue. *What a cheap motive*, Mark thought, *for doing anything*. Better to do it because the thing needs doing or because others' welfare needs for it to be done. Besides, that God is your *idea* of God, which may mean you are pleasing some ennobled (or twisted) extension of yourself.

When Mark and Chris first moved to Crestone, they visited all the spiritual centers here — after all, it was the only game in town — and found none without its good points. But even when he could accept their precepts, he thought them better not evoked in Sabbath meditations or Sunday prayers but quietly (or loudly) lived out in the raucous no-holds-barredness of every day. The thought occurred to Mark that religion, for someone like him, can get in the way of having a religious experience.

Rule 4: Laugh. During their wedding ceremony Chris thanked Mark for "making [her] see that life is too serious to be taken seriously."

Mark has a monthly radio program out of Alamosa, in which under the august seat of American politics he slips a whoopee cushion. For a station fund-raiser Mark was recruited at the very last minute to host the program on the air, without any time to prepare. He rushed there from his job managing the facilities at Valley View Hot Springs, where clothing for patrons is optional. Aha, that's what he'd do: radio nudity. For each twenty-dollar contribution phoned in, he would take off another piece of clothing. (Kizzen called in, offering forty dollars for the shirt and fifty for the pants.) It's radio, so how would anyone know, but Mark stripped anyway.

Rule 5: Be true to your word. Once when Mark was hitchhiking across country, he stopped at a bar in Sault Ste. Marie. Just as the bar was closing, some just-met bar buddies kindly offered Mark a place to stay. How hospitable. *Quite generous,* he thought. But their real plan was to rough up Mark and rob him. What bothered him most is that they had not kept true to their promise. Back at their house Mark had to fight for dear life, but during the fray he kept yelling, "You are not good hosts!"

Rule 6: Learn from the ancient wisdom. The Norse god Odin plucked out one eye (ordinary perception) in order to penetrate life's mysteries. As Mark tells of Odin blinding himself, he unobtrusively, playfully takes off his own glasses. Intriguing to Mark is the ancient idea of gnosis, of a knowledge beyond information, of a wisdom beyond knowledge, but he could never really understand what this wisdom knowledge might be — until he found Chris, and immediately lost her.

After their rapport that night at the cross-dressing club, what did she do but disappear. Not again: romance, falling in love, heartbreak, loss — it was a mug's game. Then he chanced to run into her on the street (in a city of ten million people!). Unfortunately, or fortunately, he was drunk and it all spilled out of him: what he expected of her — the opposite

of any game-playing — and his unfailing fidelity she would
never be without. Chris was a bit overwhelmed; this funny fellow from the bar was almost too serious. Mark felt great; he
had expressed himself, maybe for the first time ever. But where
had that outpouring come from? This must be what the an-
cients meant by gnosis: an effortless intuitive knowing beyond
ratiocination, in which the right thing to do does not have to
be reasoned out but spontaneously emerges as a by-product of
how one lives. Simply don't get in the way of it.

And rule 7 is...don't have a rule 7. Don't rule out what your
rules to live by hadn't yet realized was possible.

Mark's extemporaneously outlining his seven life rules
was more original or inventive than any particular rule he
named. His secular, everyday language camouflaged the fact
that he was at times adumbrating biblical or poetic truths. As I
regarded Mark conjuring his principles, these lines of William
Blake came to mind:

> God Appears and God is Light
> To those poor Souls who dwell in Night,
> But does a Human Form Display
> To those who Dwell in Realms of day.

❧

Imagine some recluse holed up in his crummy digs watching
scratchy DVDs of *Seinfeld* or *Breaking Bad* over and over. He
would be enacting Mark's rules of doing what he wanted and
harming no one, but toward no socially meaningful outcome.

Mark's principles come close to being value neutral, like the outline of an empty circle.

Let's watch Mark filling in the circle as he opposes the pyramid monstrosity and challenges the Colorado Air National Guard and defies a rapacious corporation. John Milton might have fought those battles (he has waged similar ones), but with shamanism and Hindu nature goddesses in his mind. Mark waged his fights without a religious crusader's mentality, under no heaven's banner, as though preserving Crestone's threatened environment was spirituality enough.

Mark versus the pyramid. A New Age group from Albuquerque decided to erect in the sacred vortex of Crestone a huge pyramid, which would honor an ethereal world-spirit named Kuthumi. Erecting that pharaonic mass here would be like building the Empire State Building beside Walden Pond. And as the Rajneeshees had in rural Oregon, the Kuthemians (Kuthemites?) might well turn a community into a cult, or into a town dominated by one. The Albuquerque group was unstoppable, though, and they would build their pyramid in Crestone without entertaining a single negative thought: otherwise the Earth would overturn on its axis.

Surprisingly, Mark agreed with them that such an important world edifice must be constructed, uncontaminated by negativity. At the POA meeting to approve the pyramid, Mark arranged to have person after person marshal negative arguments, backed by negative statistics, about the structure's negative environmental impact. Faced with such naysayers, the group's official channeler meditated all night and in the morning announced, "Let's get the hell out of here."

(Subsequently, a town ordinance limited the height of any new building.)

Mark versus the Air Force. For military testing, the Colorado Air National Guard needed an underinhabited wasteland, a scarcely populated nowhere of a place, and the San Luis Valley outside Crestone fit the bill. With test flights thundering overhead day and night, serene Crestone would soon reverberate like a war zone. Pretending that being the (voluntary) fire chief of Crestone gave him the authority, Mark bamboozled an air force general into coming to inspect the situation. Seeing the unspoiled nature here, appreciating that here was the true American majesty, the general canceled the maneuvers. He then presented Mark with a pair of astronaut's night goggles, which brought into focus a diamond-studded, ten-thousand-starred sky such as the naked eye of humans has never gazed upon. Mark thought, *I did not come to Crestone to fight these fights, but this is my reward.*

Mark versus the corporation. Crestone's biggest fight was, and always will be, about water. In that bone-dry climate, Crestone sits atop perhaps the largest untapped aquifer in the continental United States, which cities like Denver and even faraway Los Angeles covet to quench their ever more parched thirst.

In the Bistro Café (now the Desert Sage), circa twenty years ago, a stranger made Mark laugh out loud by announcing, "See that mountain out the window? Guess who owns it. You're looking at him." This little braggart will be dead in a wink of an eye, Mark thought, while that mountain will be standing there a million years from now. "The lummoxes of

Crestone will owe me one big-time," the stranger continued, "when they quit their jobs to dog-paddle in money."

That man was from American Water Development, Inc. (AWDI). Where the AWDI big shot saw himself pocketing a cool billion from the San Luis aquifer, Mark foresaw that draining the water table would ruin agriculture, put farmers out of business, and destroy the valley's ecosystem. He recalled the nearby Summitville mining disaster, in which Canadian entrepreneur Robert Friedland's gold-mining scheme spilled endless cyanide into the environment and left tax payers with a hundred-million-plus-dollar bill to clean up the catastrophe.

Mark and even more so his wife, Chris, helped organize grassroots groups to oppose this scenario of disaster. They put a referendum on the ballot to pay for the attorneys and engineering studies to counter AWDI's vast influence. Through the valley, across every social, political, cultural, and ethnic divide, Latinos, Anglos, farmers, and townspeople voted — 98.7 percent in favor — to tax themselves, to fight this seemingly unwinnable fight. Unwinnable, but after a dozen years they won. We have already heard how at the victory celebration Ralph Curtis, the Republican head of the Rio Grande Water Conservation District, joked to Mark, "You know, you weirdos from Crestone are okay." Mark's joke back in kind: "Yep. Our alien guides beamed us to save this land."

II

A theologian might dismiss Mark's seven rules as beside the point — the point, religion's point, being: to give birth or rebirth to a redeemed person, to a human reflection of the divine. Yet what if (by overall consensus) Crestone's most loving, happy, and visionary citizen observes no religion, and like Mark, is quite comfortable following no spiritual tradition?

Life may offer few pleasures better than on a sunny afternoon sitting outdoors talking of anything and everything under the sun with a wise old woman. Nothing you say will flatter Bertha Gotterup, nothing will shock her, and she will delight in you no matter what. Her cat, Hermes (to which I'm allergic), and her zaftig dachshund, Sophia, rub against me and purr and gurgle. Bertha observes, "They really like you," as though I please even the animals. Whenever you are around Bertha, Kizzen says, you feel the universe is on your side. Though she notices your flaws, she will see beyond them to a better you than you can see in yourself. Some women in Crestone study pottery with Bertha to learn pottery, of course, but even more so to learn, as it were, *Bertha*.

Once when visiting her I was so downcast (I forget why) I could barely speak. Bertha noticed my mute sadness — she notices everything — and here was the advice this eighty-plus-year-old woman gave: "Go out and have a blast! Everything you need is already within you." Bertha then outwitted my moodiness by asking me to make a list of books for her to read. In my depressed monosyllables: "How long a list?" "Winter stretches ahead of us," she replied, "make it good and long." Finally, I managed to think of one book. And then another. I was back home on my turf, the written word, and aliveness shook its feathers within. Maybe Bertha's asking me for the list was no clever ploy but simply Bertha being Bertha. After a certain age, Confucius said, the sage effortlessly embodies the will of heaven. When the doleful specimen of myself left that day, instead of being relieved, Bertha commented, "What a wonderful time!" That is how she perceives time.

"How can you see everything so positively?" Bertha is sometimes asked. Her answer: "That's all there is." How many even deeply devout people can make such a claim? Bertha has made the longest journey, which began when all circumstances appeared hostile, till now, when she welcomes practically everything and is afraid of nothing (except the bears lumbering though her yard).

Bertha's beloved Crestone can be a difficult place to live, to which dreamers often migrate full of beautiful hopes and later move away, forgetting to take those hopes with them. About those would-be settlers who then exeunt, old-timers here sneer, "The mountains spit them out." As with most everything else, Bertha views it in a more favorable light. "They came here because they wanted to or needed to," she says. "And most got what they wanted, maybe in a way they didn't expect, and had no need to tarry longer."

Bertha's early life hardly lends itself to a positive interpretation. Or maybe it did, in the very beginning, in the Danish Virgin Islands, in luxuriant tropical ease. Paradise shut down when she was seven, though, when her father accidentally drowned. Her cold, aloof mother farmed Bertha out to her equally cold grandmother in Denmark, who in turn made her a ward of the state. In the gray Baltic mists Bertha barely knew where she was or who she was. During World War II she joined the underground resistance to the Nazis, witnessing more horrors than anyone still in her teens should. After the war she returned to the Virgin Islands, to be welcomed by her mother thus: "I hope you have money. I am not giving you one damned penny to sponge off me."

In time she married, had children, and enjoyed affluence — and walked away from it, when her husband treated their children cruelly. She took the children and little else as she ricocheted from the unknown to the unknown, from farming in the Northwest to smoking salmon in Alaska. After veering down so many strange and often difficult paths, anything the future offered, or failed to offer, she had lost all terror of.

Bertha read my book about discontented Westerners who find solace in the spiritual East. After reading it, she asked, "Why did those women go to Tibet and India?" Because of their gender, I answered: second-class citizens in their religion of origin, they sought to be equal in the robes of another.

"Were they second-class citizens in their own minds," Bertha probed, "or in reality?"

"In society's reality, I fear."

"And they let that hold them back?" Bertha was amazed that anyone would let herself be deterred by external prejudices and pressures. Harsh circumstances had honed in her the determination not to be limited by them. Yet semiorphaned by her father's death, cast out by her mother, rejected by her grandmother, and growing up a ward of the Danish state, she never felt she belonged anywhere, until she was nearing sixty and moved to Crestone. During her first month here she could not stop crying, a monthlong bath of tears, which washed away a lifetime of sorrows. Now when people ask her what her religion is, she answers, "I am standing on it."

Bertha found a second home here in an activity, an occupation. The first time she plunged her hands into potter's clay, she thought, *I am doing what I should be doing.* Bertha now has pieces in museums throughout the country, but pottery for her means more than income or recognition. When throwing pots, she feels a magical collaboration, the clay going from liquid to solid as she interacts with it. The clay is fluid and her hands are in a dance with it, and need to be, second by second, or the piece will be ruined. Making pottery forces her out of memories and plans and into her hands at the moment and the moment at hand.

Now comes the saddest moment of this book, as it changes from present to past tense. On Christmas Eve, 2012, quietly and without fuss, Bertha Gotterup died. She is written about here as though she were alive, because she was very much alive during most of the book's time span, and these pages refuse to consign her living vitality to a fading memory.

Once when we were talking, Bertha speculated, "Do you think this is all" — she gestured to nothing in particular as she hunted for the right word — "all part of a scheme?" *A scheme?* I had no answer, if there is one. Perhaps her simply posing the question enmeshed us in a grander design. Someone like Bertha, who finds the good where others find nothing, or worse, whose life course mutated from purgatorial beginnings to a fulfilled present, and who creates beauty not just through pottery but simply by being herself — does that hint at a benevolent scheme (or if not, then perhaps no need for one)?

Bertha can express those simple sentiments that great minds fail to say. One year at the Strongs' Christmas party, Maurice asked what everyone hoped from the new year, and eloquent were the rejoinders. When it came to be Bertha's

turn, she merely said, "Couldn't we just touch each other?"
When she heard the young 17th Karmapa, a figure of majestic
presence, speak in Boulder, while others wanted to prostrate
before him, her response was, "I wish I could cook dinner for
him." Her responses are so uncontrivedly kind, that I once
thought to ask her, "Bertha, what is kindness?"

"Kindness?" She reflected a moment and then said,
"Kindness is being."

Sometimes I suspected that Bertha's ordinary state of
being might not be all that ordinary (perhaps no one's is).
She appeared attuned, as certain animals are, to colors, smells,
and stimuli normally outside our usual range of perceptions.
One afternoon, for example, I found her working on an ele-
gant ceramic urn, imprinting it with nature's harvest of leaves
and berries. Bertha kept checking the photograph of the deceased young woman whose ashes the urn would house. "No,
not right yet," she would shake her head, and then return to
the clay. "Did you ever meet the deceased girl in the photograph?" I asked. "Yes, I rocked her in my arms when she was
a baby," Bertha answered. "I surmised then she was an old
soul and would not have a long life." How could anyone surmise *that*?

I was struck that in a book Bertha loaned me, *Black Elk
Speaks* (alas, too late to return it now), she had underlined
only one sentence. As a boy Black Elk had a dream or vision of kindly grandfathers walking toward him. When in
the vision one grandfather spoke, however, Black Elk started
to tremble. This is the sentence that Bertha underlined: <u>His
voice was very kind, but I shook all over with fear now, for</u>

I knew that these were not old men, but the Powers of the
World.

Bertha is — was — a kindly old grandmother who noticed what others overlooked and in the end found most of it
positive and re-created its ineffability in forms of clay. She
was far too gentle and humorous, though, to be a power of
the world, unless disguised to everybody, including herself,
she was.

III

How do you deepen spirituality — deepen, that is, your feelings of connection, your spontaneous inclination to help,
your vision of a vaster whole — other than by going to
church, meditating, doing good deeds, or praying to God?
One (John Milton) led people far from their homes out into
these mountains to effect that inner upgrade. Another (Bertha)
stayed quietly at home, as though the earth beneath her was
religion enough. One (Mark Jacobi) finds within the local
confines of little Crestone a microcosm of involvement with all
humankind. Another (Ralph Abrams) widens those confines,
whether by going on retreats or, after being mayor, starting an
internet telecom company. The good life is by each one differently constructed. What talking with his neighbors is for Mark,
tantric snakebites are for John; what Buddhist sabbaticals are
for Ralph, making pottery was for Bertha. John and Ralph
ransacked spiritual traditions — Buddhism, shamanism, Hinduism, Taoism, Jungian psychology — to fulfill their innate
human potential, while Mark and Bertha attempted it without
religious assists or any spiritual supplements.

What common denominator then, if any, exists among these four? All of them, John and Bertha and Mark and Ralph — instead of acting out a script handed to them by their familial religion — devised their own scenarios by which to carry on this strange business of being a mind and body on Earth. If all human history were compacted into a single day, then only in the past minute have a few out-of-the-mold prototypes like them had to become, as it were, the author of their own lives. On a planet too overcrowded to allow rampant individuality, ironically this may be the assignment for many individuals today: whether innovatively religious (John and Ralph) or not recognizably religious at all (Mark and Bertha), each must personally cobble together the meaning and purpose that once the priest or rabbi sounded from the pulpit on high.

Only a short time ago — a moment on our history-in-a-day clock (or two or so centuries in human time) — this globe, this Earth, existed much as it always had. Then overnight it changed, it became cancerously overpopulated, depleted in resources, coughing from a dysfunctional climate, reeling from one environmental meltdown to the next. Compared to the dinosaurs' hundred-million-year reign, the human cohort may have a short run of it, turning off the lights as they go. As long as men presume they can own mountains, the greed of the short term will trample the necessities of the long run. The counter to this for-profit wreckage is, possibly, the idea of not-for-profit sacredness.

Sacredness used to be the monopoly of religion, but — judging by Bertha and Mark — a secular sacredness may now be in the works. Mark was joking that alien guides had instructed him to protect this valley, but something had. Asked about her religion, Bertha points to the ground beneath her. These four ordinary human beings (or sort of ordinary) are pioneers in a new territory that might be called *postreligion*: forging hallowed understanding — even where there was none before — as they generate their own "seven principles to live by" and consider sacrosanct the Earth on which they stand. They begin the answer to the question, How do we live in the twenty-first century, so that there may be a twenty-second?

PART III

POSTRELIGIOUS VARIETIES OF EXPERIENCE IN CRESTONE

6. An Ordinary Thursday in Crestone

"The mass of men lead lives of quiet desperation," Thoreau famously wrote. Though not exactly desperate, many feel trapped in decent but dull existences where the wondrous is relegated to Harry Potter, while they can imagine nothing extraordinary happening to themselves. Is humdrum life an undercurrent hum in Crestone, too?

Life humdrum? There are Buddhist books with titles like *Nothing Special* or *After the Ecstasy, the Laundry*. I might buy a book titled *How Never to Do Laundry Again*, except (see chapter 3 with shirts of spots and stains) I sort of figured that one out for myself. Every day dear souls are jumping off bridges because *nothing special* stretches out before them tediously, endlessly.

Over the years some of those craving *something special* have moved to Crestone on the chance that it might be found there. All those spiritual centers, tucked away in the mountains — did they not hint at a reality different from that found elsewhere? With some such anticipation, they relocated there, expecting the curtains of the mundane to part. But when they did (or didn't) part, what was often revealed was the all too familiar, at a different altitude and with a different zip code.

It is Thursday night. What happens on an ordinary Thursday evening in Crestone? Poker night! Next to Ralph's, in a house so plain a third-grader might have drawn it — squares and rectangles; frame, door, windows — sitting around the table are a dozen hardworking men and a couple of women, with dealt cards in hand. "I be ashamed to confess it," one old fellow says to me, "but I wait all week for this." Only a few miles away lie the spiritual centers, but here there is little talk about religion, and that not of a very high order. "Why do Jews have big noses?" one man asks. His joke elicits no takers. "Because air is free." The man may have never known a Jew (except Ralph); it's garden-variety small-town bigotry. Yet something else, homespun and easy and tender, curls like smoke around the table. The youngest player is an adolescent with mental problems. Elsewhere he'd be kept at home, but here he can play along; nobody minds. His mom comes to pick him up but sees him enjoying himself. Quietly she slips away, to come back later.

It could have been poker night anywhere. Thinking back over the day, I realize that everything had been ordinary, but with a slight Crestone twist.

For instance, morning coffee at the Bliss. At the next table over, a forlorn, homely fellow was moaning about how he had left a woman a phone message, asking her for a date. Now he was in agony: Will she accept? Will she like him? Will his nervousness spoil everything? His friend was all-knowing reassurance: "Don't have expectations.... Whatever happens will be the right thing.... Treat what happens as your teacher." The forlorn lover nodded. "Yeah, I guess that's right." In former times frantic suitors in the frenzied tumult of lust and love did not calm themselves by being so New Age wise. They raged, they cursed, they despaired instead of loftily relabeling bad outcomes as disguised good ones. Eavesdropping, I wondered: Is faux enlightenment the default mode of conversation in Crestone?

Human love is risky; what you can count on is vegetables. After leaving the café I stopped to buy produce at the truck stand between town and the Baca. An older farm couple from the Valley, Kent and Suzanne, get up before dawn, load a ton of produce into their truck, and drive several hours to Crestone to sell it there every Thursday, during the warm months. The one other customer there, scruffy and scraggily, introduced himself as Chuck and announced to Suzanne that he was an old soul who has reincarnated to save the planet. The Dalai Lama or Pope Francis, maybe, but Chuck? Suzanne, the good farmwife, responded, "Really? I never heard of that before." Chuck is what people elsewhere mean about Crestone when they say *Crestone*! The ordinary may be unordinary here only in how the mundane occasionally gets mixed up with the incredible.

Death, for example, occurs everywhere, yet Crestone's End of Life Project may be unlike anything anywhere else. The End of Life volunteers arrange outdoor cremations with only the Earth below and heaven above, after first taking care of the deceased's body and comforting the grieving and helping them devise a meaningful ceremony. Funerals can cost a small fortune in America; here all this is done for the minimal price of the firewood.

This Thursday night the End of Life Project was holding its monthly meeting: only three miles separate poker night, where the stakes were play, from this gathering, where the stakes were mortality. Volunteer organizations, not hemmed in by workplace rules, can be a free-for-all for egos, but at this meeting nobody's vanity was preening, calling for attention. Death was approached in a commonsensical manner, with so much intelligence devoted to small details. Should we put up finials on the cremation ground's fence? How would it affect the birds landing on them? And how to raise the mighty sum, fifteen hundred dollars, that the finials would cost? Death is not a small detail, though, but it triggers unconscious reactions and deep fears. Even while they deliberated minutiae, the volunteers planned a retreat to explore how their attitudes about their own deaths, their bogs of unexamined emotions, affected their work. An End of Life Project like Crestone's should be widely available, yet cremations in the open air, unmanaged by professional morticians, are unheard of or are outlawed in most of America.

So the Native American Indians were right: Crestone is a good place to die. And it is also not the worst place, while living, to be down on your luck. Today I noticed a flyer for an upcoming benefit sponsored by Neighbors Helping Neighbors, a volunteer organization that helps individuals in Crestone needing help. At last year's benefit, for the entertainment, some macho guys embarrassed themselves by singing in frilly dresses, while craftspeople donated their wares for auction. Any funds so collected were to benefit Nancy Ozukai, a former ballet dancer — ballet not being kind to one's joints — who to keep her legs mobile and herself out of a wheelchair, required unaffordable hip-replacement surgery. When Nancy approached Neighbors Helping Neighbors, they had only one question for her: "What took you so long?"

"We have Neighbors Helping Neighbors," one local wit observed. "And then we have Neighbors Burning Neighbors." Neither group comes out of the twenty-five spiritual centers here, but those centers provide a background atmosphere, a soil, where such ideas, such humanity, more easily take root and bloom.

After stocking up on healthful goodies at the roadside stand, I slowed down when passing Mark Elliott's house and stopped. He would likely be busy editing his latest documentary, but also too English-polite to say so. Having found Mark number one (Jacobi)'s principles so interesting, on the spur of the moment I decided to ask Mark number two (Elliott) what his were. Specifically, I wondered how he could embody such an oxymoron — a shrewd realist noting everyone's follies but with such a good heart, liking them regardless and always willing to come to their aid.

Mark's principle, it turned out, was to have no principles, at least not dogmatic, moral ones. He mistrusted people who claimed to be guided by high-minded ethics. His mother, an upper-class English Catholic, was highly principled — she would never tell a lie, for instance — but was also cool and uncompassionate. His father, a well-known Cold War spy, thought principles were fancy notions you crumpled up and tossed into the wastepaper basket but nonetheless was always moved by empathy to be of help.

"But Mark," I persisted, "let me ask you this. What have you gotten out of your long years of Buddhist practice?" If he wasn't going to talk principles, what about some mystical razzle-dazzle, the wonders of the greater Self or awakened mind that make principles seem a rote Sunday school lesson? Mark's response was down-to-earth. "The purpose of any religion," he said, "is to make you a more decent, generous person, which is worth more than magical powers. If you meditate twenty years in a cave and have enlightened realizations for breakfast, and yet are not a whit kinder, better have passed the time in a pub."

Be kinder — is that it? An ordinary Thursday in Crestone was becoming a bit too ordinary.

Did anything at all unusual mark that Thursday — anything that was not happening in every city and hamlet across America? One small occurrence, though of no consequence, comes to mind.

That afternoon I was in a bad mood. I was coming down with the flu. I couldn't collapse into bed, for I had an appointment so far up the mountain I worried that the "Pimpmobile" (my ancient rented Mercedes) might not chug to such vertical heights. Besides, I hadn't been able to reach the man by phone and felt certain he had forgotten about our meeting. Driving along unfamiliar roads in that mountainous sprawl, I lost my bearings. Finally I knocked at the door of the only house in sight to ask directions. How — Crestone is not that populous — could the woman who answered not have heard of his street?

She said I was welcome to use her landline,* though

---

*   Cell phones at that time did not work well in Crestone, and GPS systems were usually more lost than I was.

— another waste of time since he wouldn't be there — but, surprise, on the second ring he answered and said he was waiting for me, and it was only a few corners and turns away. Putting down the phone I looked around. Had I strayed into grandma's cottage in some old fairy tale? Architecturally, the house resembled an oversize mushroom, erected around a tree trunk extending from floor to ceiling. In it a dozen women of every age, shape, and description milled around. "Are you," I asked, "uh, some sort of group?" They all laughed. Like witches, good witches, in a fairy tale, they gathered monthly to prepare herbal remedies. The medicine they had just prepared — *miracle de Dieu!* — was for flu, and they poured me some into a bottle,* which (they said) would fix me right up. Just being in their midst was a kind of fix-me-up. Did I really have to go to my appointment? Couldn't I just sit quietly in a corner and worship them? Politely, if reluctantly, I bade them goodbye, though in a mood much improved. When I later described this incident, friends commented, "Oh, a typical Crestone experience."

That coven of good witches who were not witches, gathering, gossiping, and cooking together, did not bend any of the rules of commonly accepted reality. In that sense they — and everything else that happened that Thursday — fell well within the boundaries of the commonplace.

Would it not be interesting, though, if some of what transpires in Crestone did not conform to common, everyday

---

* Ingredients: skullcap, uvaursi, mullein, white oak bark, lobelia, comfrey, black walnut, marshmallow root, wormwood, garlic, honey, vinegar, and glycerin.

assumptions? Yet if 92.5 percent* of what occurs in Crestone is just what occurs everywhere, the remaining chapters will touch on that other 7.5 percent. We shall detour behind the cozy scenes of the everyday, and of everyday religion, too, to delve into "strange sights, Things invisible to see" (John Donne), though possibly lying quite near, swept under familiarity's old carpet. In our probing we may encounter saints and sinners, possibilities and high jinks, and extraordinary if elusive matters that do indeed appear *something special*. And once the laundry is done and put away, we might even brush lightly against the ecstasy.

---

*   This percentile statistic is made up — either an apt symbol or a bad guess.

7. A Sacred Relationship to the Natural World?

N o book was holding my attention. "What should I read?" I complained to Bertha. "Here," she said, and handed me a paperback but warned, "You won't be able to put it down."

Back at home, I realized the challenge wasn't whether I could put it down but whether I would ever pick it up.

Its title was intriguing enough: *Of Water and the Spirit*, and its author boasted a name mellifluous as water running over stone — Malidoma Somé. But its subtitle seemed to consign it to the genre of tribal voodoo: *Ritual, Magic, and Initiation in the Life of an African Shaman*. Africa, don't bother with Google maps, is a long way from Crestone. As for shamanism, I barely knew enough to dismiss it as nature religion dating from long ago. I did open Bertha's/Malidoma's book that night in bed long enough to surmise that for shamans *natural* and *supernatural* were not opposed but nearly synonymous, sharing the same earthy address.* However, more I

---

* Apropos: "We Sioux spend a lot of time thinking about everyday things, which in our mind are mixed up with the spiritual.... We Indians live in a world of symbols and images where the spiritual and the commonplace are one." — John Lame Deer, a Sioux-Lakota medicine man who came many times to Crestone.

cannot say for I soon drifted off into unconscious night, into a most unshamanic sleep.

An Accidental Shaman?

At that time I was staying at Neil Hogan's house, a house he'd built single-handedly, neat and trim down to the last detail. Neil was no shaman but rather a good ol' boy from West Virginia. Except, that is, for his intelligence and his having worked in Africa. Too grand for his taste, Neil had built the house for his sister Brady, and I was house-sitting while she was on retreat in Nepal. When Crestone winters finally froze him out of his tent, Neil nailed together a tiny one-room cabin without electricity or running water for himself. Evidently that's too grand for him, too, for at that time he was building a half-submerged greenhouse with a dirt floor so he could sleep directly on the earth again. His West Virginia buddies might find Neil's housekeeping preferences strange, but a shaman wouldn't.

Last year Neil visited a beach at the Jersey Shore with Tsoknyi's "man Friday," Lama Tashi. They were lazing on the sand when Neil had to urinate. The largest toilet in the world lay conveniently right before him, and Neil headed into the ocean to pee. But Lama Tashi yelled, "No!" Tashi was not worried that Neil would pollute the water (at the Jersey Shore? Hardly possible.) but that he would offend the *nagas*, the serpent-like spirits that protect bodies of water. Back in Crestone, when Neil is by the stream near his house and needs to piss, he first requests permission from whatever spirits or energies inhabit the land. Even if those spirit-energies are only imaginary (a shaman would not make that distinction), doing so fosters his awareness of and respect for the Earth.

Neil has reminded me several times not to leave the door open, lest flies and bugs get in. Homeowners are fussy, but it turned out that Neil was concerned not for his house but for the flies, who might get trapped indoors. He has some sci-fi-looking device for catching flies alive, and when it does he whirls the device about like a church censor, saying prayers over the flies, before releasing them outside. In Buddhism he and the flies were now considered to have some connection, which will last through future lifetimes. Neil's respect for all living beings, his honoring the *nagas*, his invoking the spirit of the land, resemble shamanism, but without the name.

His West Virginian buddies — say, like the one who keeps his own permanent table at a Denver strip club — would howl if they heard about Neil's rescuing flies or requesting the spirits' permission to pee. Neil's approach to his surroundings, despite his old buddies' derision, carries a certain benefit: it charges the dull, heavy *thingness* of daily life with vibrancy and interconnection. Animals, trees, and streams become Neil's fellow travelers.

Unlike some shaman wannabes, Neil does not ingest ayahuasca, the South American hallucinogenic, or any other drugs (or alcohol); he eats healthfully, rises early, and works hard, and in his late fifties appears fit as a thirty-year-old. Next to him I look like the seven deadly sins having a bad day. Usually people who housesit sister Brady's home have embarked on serious retreats themselves. When Neil found me in the house drinking beer and reading a book called *Naked* (by David Sedaris), I felt like a drunk congressman caught with his pants down.

Neil's shamanism without a name does come with its practices, though. First, as mentioned, he practically lives out-of-doors, more at home there than in his home. Second, he connects what his eyes see with what his heart feels. Opening one's gaze wide and then wider (unnatural for humans but natural for animals) has a way of stopping thought, and then what's beheld more easily migrates into, or is felt inside, oneself. Observed wide-eyed and felt afresh, nature gleams as though newly minted.

Once when Neil was away from Crestone, I asked a couple, Rob and Rachel Olds, who were staying at Brady's house, when Neil was due back. "With him you never know," Rachel laughed. "Last time on his way home, he passed an accident on the highway in which the driver was badly hurt. Neil checked into a motel for two weeks to take care of her." Shamans enter unknown situations, forget themselves, and penetrate the other's situation and try to effect a healing. Though not a shaman, Neil seems up for at least part of the job description.

Four Different Relationships to Nature

Logically, there appear to be four possible relationships that we can have to the non-man-made world.

First possibility: No relationship at all. For the first time in history, most people's, aka city folk's, interaction with nature now consists of hardly more than turning on the windshield wipers or putting on a snow parka. Fish, fruits, and vegetables — you mean those aren't grown at the supermarket? The insouciant New York poet Frank O'Hara declared that he could not enjoy a leaf of grass unless it was surrounded by concrete.

While we blithely ignore her, however, nature may fail to return the courtesy. Let some catastrophe in nature befall (Fukushima, hurricanes like Harvey and Irma) or just let it rain nonstop for two solid weeks, and our proud spirits sink, drenched. Crestone numbers among the steadily fewer places left where the majority of people still have an active relation to nature, or at least want one.

Possibility two: Subject versus object. For shrewd investors (subject), nature (object) is too juicy a plum not to be plucked. Shrewd billionaire Robert Friedland's plum, as noted earlier, was gold strip-mining in Colorado, a scheme that left him richer but left the mountainside an environmental nightmare. Dreading a similar scenario in their backyard, many folks here feared and fought AWDI's schemes for draining the San Luis aquifer. The aquifer was an object to AWDI but for Crestonians a subject, part of what made here *here*.

The third possibility: Complementary; allies. For the environmentalists of Crestone and the surrounding valley (Chris Canaly, Ceal Smith, Joe Maestas, Pauline Washburn, Matthew Crowley, Andrea Trujillo Guajaro, et al.) the route between our inner psyches and external nature is a two-way street. To traverse that street is precisely why John Milton's students come to Crestone and go on a Sacred Passage.

One of John's students, Douglas Canterbury-Counts, explains how a Sacred Passage works. A silent tête-à-tête with the natural surroundings over wordless days empties out his habitual mental repertoire. On retreat Doug is allowed no books or writing materials; his mind forfeits its familiar intellectual props. During one Sacred Passage Doug found himself reading and rereading, as though it were a profound philosophical text, the label on a tuna can.

Then after three days his mind no longer needed to distract itself. He was transferring to a new campsite when he noticed a mountain lion perched on a nearby rock, intently observing him. Across the barrier of species, he and the mountain lion stared into each other's eyes. Though frightened, John finally stuttered to the lion, "I must borrow your land to complete my retreat. I will take good care of it." The lion then lay down.

The next day a rough, don't-fuck-with-me hombre drove up, hauled some equipment out of his truck, and began chipping away at a gigantic rock crystal, probably to sell the pieces as souvenirs. The sole rule on John's land is, if you accidentally move a stone, put it back in its place. If any rock could be considered sacred, Doug thought, that giant crystal was it. Recalling the mountain lion, Doug emulated its fierce spirit, as he swelled up and roared at the man, "This is government property you are destroying [it wasn't], and I shall call the rangers" [they wouldn't have come]. The man backed away and scooted off in his car, nearly as nervous as if an actual mountain lion had threatened him. (Later Doug saw that where the man's car tires had left ruts, dozens of lion tracks crisscrossed over them.) John had not instructed him about totem animals, so Doug was left to figure out on his own how the fauna around him might also be — what? — omens? Or more than omens, allies?

Possibility four: Confluence. The kind of trials Doug faced on his weeklong retreats were by now a distant memory for the Crestone woman we know as Galaxy. For her, after doing so many Sacred Passages, they presented hardly more challenge than an extended picnic. Why not then multiply the benefits of a seven-day solo retreat by four and make her home in the wilds for a whole month? Which was precisely what Galaxy did this year in the mountains above Crestone.

The first seven days flew by: the rocks, the trees, the dark nights alone felt like a reunion with old friends. But after the familiar seven days an unexpected mental chatter began in her head — a nonstop interior monologue, jabbering, mumbling, nattering — and she became like a madwoman unable to quit muttering to herself. Galaxy's physical movements, too, registered as loud, a disturbance of the peace, so that wherever she moved birds and animals shied clear of. In the middle of nature, she had scared nature away.

Yet, as unexpectedly as it had begun, the crazed cacophony within gradually subsided, having exhausted itself. The birds came back, the bugs came back, the rhythms of nature resumed and became her rhythms, too. A moth, instead of fleeing her brusque human movement, crawled into the folds of her dress to make its home there. Sitting under a tree, she felt a part of it, like one of its roots or branches. Previously Galaxy had suffered from low self-esteem, which undermined her relationships since she doubted she was worth affection or devotion. Nature, she felt, was now accepting her, which mitigated any feelings of inferiority.

Now in a hyperstate with senses grown razor-sharp, Galaxy began to experience below-the-radar perceptions that were not dreams, though they half seemed so. Weeks of quiet passed, with her only companions the squirrels and the birds. In such prolonged solitude she could not tell for certain how much was real and how much was her imagination's handiwork. It seemed almost as though the space inside her mind and the space outside her were continuations of the same space, and through it, as in some primal medium, everything — ideas, emotions, energy — concentrated and densified into human perception. Along with the noonday heat, starry nights, wind, and rocks, she too now figured into nature's blueprint, its template (or so it felt). If Doug's week alone in the wild transformed him, Galaxy's month in it left the world for her transformed.

What did she gain from it, what did she take home from her retreat besides mosquito bites? Back down in Crestone (after her month solo, a veritable New York City of bustling metropolisdom), Galaxy speculated that the answer to such a question might be: nothing tangible. But the need for a specific identity, or to take on some project to justify herself — she no longer felt that. The urge to do more retreats or spiritual training — that too was gone. The monthlong retreat, that exercise in independence, should have matured her, but if anything she now felt more childlike, or even animal-like, but a child or animal that can function perfectly well in the complex adult human world.

It seems a pity that Galaxy had to embark on this potentially life-changing adventure when she was feeling quite ill.

To begin with, she was in the midst of menopause, with all its metabolic shenanigans. And she had come down with a serious case of the flu. In addition to menopause and the flu, she had an autoimmune disease, the prescription steroids for which kept her from going blind but made her feel even sicker. During the days leading up to the retreat she bemoaned, *Why do I have to feel bad just now?*

The obstacles she faced during that retreat may make it a kind of parable for our time. America's (and the developed world's) long, fat years of unparalleled prosperity appear to be ending, and henceforth accomplishment will be achieved despite hardships, not luxuriously *because of* but defiantly *in spite of.* In spite of menopause, flu, and the noxious steroids, Galaxy achieved something worthwhile: a sense of being accepted at some very basic level, of being an integral part of what is, which in turn fused her self-acceptance. The fewer the obstacles, perhaps the less durable the triumph?

An Aside (in Which We Attend Both a Sweat Lodge and a Medicine Wheel Ceremony)

In retrospect, my greatest regret about my time in Crestone is that I never ventured on one of John's nature retreats. John was always encouraging me to, enticing me with the offer of his "maharajah tent." Why didn't I? Two reasons, I guess. First, I wouldn't have known what to do. (but John would surely have given me guidance.) Second, high up on the mountainside, it would have been cold, too cold.

However, I did taste some of the shamanic flavor of

Crestone, for example, when I took part in a Blackfoot sweat lodge held at the autumn equinox. Before doing so, I first visited Dan Retuta so that he could instruct me on how to participate in the sweat.

With his ponytail and smooth bronze skin, Dan could easily be mistaken for an American Indian himself. Although born in the Philippines, he has immersed himself in other spiritualities, particularly Native American ones. His own preferred practice is to sit in silence with old Native American women: their mere presence attunes him, he feels, to unspoken truths. During a recent sweat lodge here, hot almost beyond endurance, while others were fainting or collapsing out of the tent, Dan sat as calm as an old tribal chief, with eyes closed and the sweetest smile on his face, not even sweating. In Sun Dance ceremonies he can hang suspended by hooks in his flesh and never cry out or seem even to mind the pain.

As we discussed the upcoming sweat lodge, Dan said that should the heat become unbearable, just vamoose out of the tent, no shame or blame attached. Before exiting, though, I must say loudly *mee tah koo yah seen* ("me-tak-i-ah-sin"), which means "all my relations," flesh, fish, and fowl, human or spirit, manifested or unmanifested. By chanting the phrase, I thus acknowledged my shamanic kinship with all of living creation. Dan wrote *mee tah koo yah seen* on a sheet of paper for me to remember it. After the phrase he put an *!* and after that *!* followed another *!* and then *another !*, and after the *!!!* shot a fourth *!*.

I studied Dan as he spoke of the kinship of all creatures in the web of all things. Here was someone for whom life's interconnectedness was not a beautiful theory but a living, thrilling reality. Dan's *!!!!* was one of the most memorable things I ever heard in Crestone, although, since they were punctuation, I never heard them at all.

The sweat lodge proved a Crestonian kind of event, so I'll say a word or two about it, even though (a) I mainly embarrassed myself at it and (b) I nearly died, or it felt like it — things that ordinarily can spoil a day's outing. I had done sweats before in California, but this was not California. Not at all.

As we milled about beforehand there was a lot of joking and wisecracking: "You won't feel a drop of perspiration." But when Lorain Fox Davis, who is part Lakota, called out, "Better start saying your prayers now," it sounded like no joke. Not long in the lodge, I was plunged into the heat and darkness of the damned. My lungs seemed to be inhaling barely any air. Yet Dan Retuta sat across from me completely unruffled, eyes closed, wearing a smile of unsurpassing sweetness, as though in his own realm — or galaxy. But for me, in the claustrophobic, torrid darkness, I felt in place of my body only animal terror. My brain, stunned, inoperative, fumbled for some thought and found — blank, nothing — blank, nothing — even as the temperature approached low oven heat. I was suffocating, panicking. There welled up within me (less in words than in mute sensation) the command *Get out!* I mumbled apologetically, "Mee tah koo yah seen. I am fine but my pitiable body isn't," and collapsed out of the tent.

I was about to drink from the water hose, but a woman called out, "If you drink, you cannot go back into the sweat." Go back? Not in my plans. I put the hose down anyway, and in the shade of a tree I lay my wimpy self down.

A sweat has four doors, or rounds, and just before the

fourth Lorain's husband, David, supposedly seventy but with the swagger of a twenty-five-year-old, called me to come back in. Did I dare? He situated me near the entrance, so that any illicit air that trickled in I'd get the benefit of. I tried to recall some phrase or mantra to keep my frightened brain distracted, but crazily the only words that came were *thank you*. In the claustrophobic tent, fast and faster I kept repeating *thankyouthankyouthankyou*. Quite unexpectedly David announced that the sweat was over. Already? Had he radically abbreviated it so I could be part of it? If so, what a thoughtful act of kindness this was. Afterward there was a big feast at Lorain and David's. But I hadn't earned a right to be there, so I slinked off, without anyone noticing.

The next day there was a Native American Medicine Wheel ceremony to honor the land and pray that it be protected against corporate interests (like Halliburton) that would chew it up and spit it out. Some of the same folks who were at the sweat would be there, and though they would say nothing, I would be embarrassed by my poor showing yesterday. *Ah, what the hell*, I thought, *I'll go anyway*.

At the ceremony we formed a great circle, and into its center Lorain summoned a couple of people to offer the invocations. For some reason she called me to represent Father Sun. Probably her reason was like David's yesterday: to make me feel esteemed in my own eyes. I did feel kind of proud, like a bit actor who'd landed a role on Broadway. After the ceremony Lorain said to me, "Father Sun? Impressive." "Yes," I agreed. "Some pretty big shoes to fill."

Later I ran into David, and what he said could not have

sounded odder: "I'm glad you got from the sweat what you came for."

Had I? What had I expected from it? Suddenly yesterday's — and today's — events appeared in a different light. About the guys participating in the men's sweat, rarely have I been with a group that I liked better. They were good men who built their own homes and repaired their old cars themselves; they had the integrity of elements of nature; they were self-deprecating, with their jokes being at their own expense. They had, it turns out, noticed when I had slipped away. Will, who had managed the sweat and kept its fire hell-hot, now asked, "Why weren't you at the banquet last night? Did somebody offend you?" I gave the expected comeback, "Just you, Will, just you." Twice kindness had shown its simple face, when David cut short the sweat's final round and today when Lorain summoned me to be Father Sun. My ego, that vainglorious thing, had been humbled and my ego had been consoled.

Even if I hadn't consciously reentered the shaman's interconnected web of all things, I felt affinity for these people and knew that we were joined together in some larger undertaking. Or to quote Dan Retuta: "!!!!"

An Englishman Goes Native (American)

Remember Galaxy's ordeals? They hardly compare with what shamans like Malidoma Somé (in the book Bertha loaned me) endured in the wilderness, facing terrors both external and internal, which alter them to their core. However, no Native

American shamans or chiefs are left around Crestone to tell us about nature spirituality.

And maybe they could not have told us anyway. For centuries Ute, Lakota, Navajo, and Hopi, made religious pilgrimages to these, their sacred mountains, yet reportedly their languages have no word for *religion*. How could any one specific word encompass what for them pervades everything? Native Americans came here to pray, as Lorain Fox Davis noted, but prayer for them meant something different than it does for, say, a Christian. In Lakota, for example, prayer (*wacekiye*) implies "to seek connection to." The Native Americans connected to these mountains in such a way that rendered church, faith, and even religion unnecessary.

Though none live here today, in the (largely unwritten) annals of Native American history nowhere have more great American Indians stood on the same spot than on the ground of Crestone. A long parade of Indian luminaries animated Crestone only recently. In the 1980s and '90s Hanne Strong enticed to Crestone a veritable who's-who of Native American chiefs, medicine men, and shamans — Red Ute, Wallace Black Elk, Thomas Banyacya, both Sr. and Jr., Grandfather David, James Kootshongsie, Wallace "Mad Bear" Anderson, Leon Shenandoah, Chief Arvol Looking Horse, Harrison Begay, Red Cloud, Chief Robert Smallboy, White Rainbow, Leading Earth Man, White Sun Man, Little Turtle, Sam Moves Camp, Ellen Moves Camp, Rudy Runs Above, Mike Sierra Burns Prairie, Yellow Bird, Burton Pretty On Top, Willy Big Bull, Chief Peter O'Chiese, Princess Little Star, Tony Starlight, Doris Starlight, Alex White Plume, Chief Eugene Steinhauer, Bobby Woods, Paul Tohlakai, Sequoyah

Trueblood, Tellus Goodmorning, N. Scott Momaday, John Eagle Day, Winona LaDuke, Leading Earth Woman, Jamake Highwater, Tu Moonwalker, Moises and Benki Piyãko, Brontoi, Hunbatz Men, Maya Itza, Jerome Fourstar, Janet McCloud, Jose Lucero, John (Fire) Lame Deer, and many others — to transmit their worldviews here.

Nobody appreciated the quiet otherness that these Native American chiefs imported to Crestone more than Mark Elliott. In the 1980s Mark had relocated from Boulder to Crestone, so he joked, to get away from Buddhists. (Today that would be like moving to Brooklyn to get away from hipsters.) Exhausted by Chögyam Trungpa's dharma circus in Boulder, Mark longed for someplace more tranquil, a milieu untried. The Indians who came here whom he befriended — Henry Crow Dog, his son Leonard Crow Dog, Sam Moves Camp, Lame Deer, Leonard Shenandoah, Arvol Looking Horse — became for him that something else. They made the best company, never in a hurry, always laughing, ever in good humor. A few Indians Mark got to know, such as Lame Deer, expressed realizations he thought similar to those of the greatest Tibetan masters like Dilgo Khyentse or the 16th Karmapa.

Early on, Henry Crow Dog invited Mark to the Lakota Reservation to film their secret Sun Dance ceremony. Mark declined: the heart was willing, but the bank account was empty. Then two weeks before the ceremony, Crow Dog appeared to him in a dream, summoning him. Mark woke, thinking, *Go I must*, and luckily he found a cameraman willing to accompany him and also able to finance the trip. Approaching the reservation, Mark recognized the landscape he had seen in his dream. Nearing the reservation, he could hear the drumming before he could see it, and he could sense the vibrations even earlier. Mark was pleased that he had come after all; the Lakota elders, anything but. Despite Crow Dog's invitation, it would be sacrilegious, they told him, to film a Sun Dance ceremony. With time thus on his hands, Mark began doing sweat lodges every day, taking peyote, immersing himself in reservation life.

Back in Crestone, that connection deepened as Mark participated in native ceremonies such as the *yuwipi* or "spirit calling." These ceremonies often were held in the Baca townhouse condominiums, not one of nature's wilder places. *Yuwipi* literally means "they tie him up," and a holy man, Sam Moves Camp, would be tied up and wrapped in a blanket, in a completely darkened room.* Something otherworldly (for lack of a better word), an evanescent presence, was soon felt in the room. Mark, who is not overly susceptible to suggestion, claims he could see swirling white lights beneath the ceiling. Mark pondered those lights — had he fallen asleep? was he hallucinating? — as he drove home.

When Mark went to brush his teeth that night, he was astonished to see that his teeth were all black, as black as that ceremony room had been. Mark had been feeling ill and suddenly he felt inexplicably well, better than well, and he continued to feel this exceptionally well when his teeth returned to being even whiter. He wondered if a less tangible cause-and-effect, a different kind of healing, had occurred. Mark is a proper Englishman, the grandson of Sir Claude Aurelius

----

* For a description of this healing ritual, see the Jesuit priest William Stolzman's *How to Take Part in Lakota Ceremonies*, William K. Powers's *Yuwipi*, or Eagle Man (Ed McGaa)'s *Mother Earth Spirituality*.

Elliott, the headmaster of Eton. Sir Claude had known everybody who was anybody; Mark knew Lakota healing spirits or energies masquerading as flashing white lights. The progression from grandfather to grandson constitutes a thousand-year journey, backward.

As much as he enjoyed his Native American friends, Mark sometimes felt he was trying to cross a moat of irrevocable difference. Things that meant something quite obvious to him might have a meaning utterly otherwise for them. One evening Henry Crow Dog rambled on and on about himself, to Mark's dismay: no Englishman would so gauchely monopolize the conversation talking about himself. Later Mark learned that Lakotas rarely speak about themselves, and Henry's doing so was his telling Mark that he trusted him. Another time, when the subject happened to be murder, a Lakota friend said that were Mark to kill him, then — reasoning that something in his Lakota friend had caused Mark to do so — his family would have to adopt Mark as one of their own. Really, not the way things were done in England.

Despite the laughing and the good times, language, Mark thought, kept them from truly conversing. European and Indian grammar and syntax are so fundamentally different as to reflect, or create, metaphysically two separate universes, in which only superficially did the same things occur. When he was last in Crestone, Sequoyah Trueblood told me that in the Lakota tongue there are no words for *my* and *mine* or *your* and *yours*. Other Native American languages can hardly express our neutral three-dimensional space or our impersonal, linear time. Instead of a background grid of space and time, living potentialities pulsate undetected, out of which, given the right combination of circumstances and rituals, an event manifests and later, when circumstances shift, it sinks back into that potentiality again. For all their goodwill for one another, Mark sensed that he and his Indian friends were mixing, or failing to mix, across an oil-and-water divide.

What, then, is the chief insight that Mark smuggled across that divide? Something, he says, not taught at English boarding schools. No ironclad distinction is to be made between animate and inanimate; these do not abide in separate realities. For Indians, even a rock possesses a spirit. For Mark the Sleeping Beauty of things thus awakened. According to his Native American friends, surrounded by what's alive, we become more alive and our dance with the world turns more vibrant, dangerous, and joyful. Even if scientifically unverifiable, this idea of a living creation invites a more sacramental relationship to it, in which the Earth will not be for sale to the highest bidder.* Before erecting the great stupa here, Mark and other Buddhists made sure that Red Ute (Ed Box), representing the Native Americans whose land this once was, gave their blessing and the permission to do so.

More than from the Shambhala Buddhists in Boulder, Mark learned from the Indians who came to Crestone how to penetrate the holy without entering a shrine or temple. He learned, too, from the Native American worldview that a

---

* Lame Deer commented tongue-in-cheek that if nature is not sacred, then it was good that the whites stole from the Indians their land: "Think of what we would have missed: the motels with their neon signs, the pawn shops, the Rock Hunter's Paradise, the go-go gals and cathouses.... If the land belonged to us there would be nothing here, only trees, grass and some animals running free. All that *real estate* would be going to waste."

human being is never alone in the universe or even in his or her little neighborhood, even if nobody else is around. Mark regrets that he did not learn Lakota, which would have permitted him entrance to that Native American reality.

I wish Mark had learned the Lakota language, too. Then through him I might vicariously know those great chiefs and shamans like Lame Deer who once passed through Crestone but no longer do. There is a shaman living in Crestone, however, although he's away at the moment. When he returns, I'll solicit from him insights into that other way of knowing.

A Possibly Authentic, Albeit White, Shaman

I didn't have to solicit too hard. John Milton returned from his recent adventure in the Yucatán eager to tell about it. The ancient mysteries are not dead, he exulted; enchantments of long ago are still happening today. And they had happened to him. Before he relates his story, perhaps I should say why John, a white dude who has worked in the White House — not your typical shamanic activity — might possibly be a shaman.

Animals are drawn to him. Wild animals bond with John almost as though he were their *totem person.* When he was swimming in Florida's Saint Sebastian River, for instance, two manatees would not depart from his side; on a beach in Baja pelicans followed after him like faithful dogs. Were shamanism a religion, instead of bearded prophets or yogis in trances, it would be manifested by animals unexpectedly appearing that deliver a message from above (or below), albeit in symbols we must learn to decode.

Other shamans recognize him as one of them. Shortly before meeting John, Brian Arthur, the Stanford economist,
got a psychic reading from an Indian woman in Canada. She
foresaw that Brian would soon encounter a great shaman, but
then she recoiled from her vision in horror. "No!" she exclaimed. "It can't be. He's — he is white!"*

He has apprenticed with many shamans. His recent trip to
Yucatán was hardly his first. The first took place *fifty-five
years ago*, when as a young environmental scientist interested in ecosystems, he ventured into areas marked "Terra
Incognita" on maps, rumored to be populated with poisonous flora, dangerous fauna, and ferocious tribes. If these
unknown tribes proved hostile, John hoped it would not be
homicidally hostile.

On his first foray there, John discovered a lost Mayan
city, but that discovery was inconsequential, he felt, compared
to being adopted by a squat, powerfully built Mayan shaman
named Bor. Once John borrowed Bor's dugout to paddle to a
beautiful island in the middle of a lake. The next morning he
awoke to find his skin turning black as though being eaten away
by acid. Panicking, he rushed to the dugout to paddle for help,
only to find that termites had gnawed a hole through the bot-
tom. Bor proved gracious about his ruined dugout. John was in
far less gracious mood, as Bor cut off the infected skin (caused
by the island's highly poisonous trees) with a dull-bladed knife.

Gradually John learned from Bor three codes that
guide the shaman through the dangers of the not-human-
circumferenced world. First, in nature nothing is isolated; an

_____

* Not entirely white. One of his grandfathers was a white United States senator,
  but the other was a Native American farmer. From them he learned two different
  kinds of power.

intertwined web of interconnection weaves everything into an interactive confluence of complementary forces. Second, our familiar, seemingly solid world is the coating of a deeper actuality. Third, to penetrate this seeming solidity in order to arrive among those subterranean forces, one must die — not literally, but not merely metaphorically, either. Rather, you endure ordeals that, if you survive them, slough off your old persona like old snakeskin, and a new self (or selflessness) is born. Only then, through this three-fold transfiguration — of nature, of understanding, and of self — can the shaman move between potentiality and phenomena, using symbols and rituals to manipulate the unseen into becoming what we can see and work with.

And now, a mere fifty-five years later, John was back from the Yucatán again, eager to tell a new tale. It goes like this....

Suppose. Suppose that the ancient Mayan cosmos is secretly still intact. Suppose its catalyzing rituals can cause latent forces within you to well up. Suppose plants and stones intangibly influence us in ways unknown, beyond observable cause-and-effect. Suppose all that, and John's experience at the ruins of Mayapán in the Yucatán may be just what he supposed it to be. Otherwise — a series of flukes, insignificant coincidences.

In Mayapán it was a beautiful day, with a flawless blue sky overhead when, scraping against a rock in his open-toed sandals, John felt his right foot begin to bleed. Recalling the ancient Mayans' belief in auspicious human sacrifices, he thought, *Why not put the blood to use?* While making his blood offering at the pyramid's altar, John sensed a presence just outside his peripheral vision.

Spinning around quickly, from exactly that angle, he spied an unusual rock barely visible in the jungle foliage. Limping over to inspect it, he determined it was not an ordinary rock but an ancient Mayan meditation seat. (Native Americans meditated? — who knew?) Because of one's angle of vision when seated on the rock, John believed he knew, from his own meditative experiences, the exact meditations those Mayans did. Furthermore, from his having worked in Asia with Tibetan refugees, he ascertained that those meditations were identical to the most advanced meditations of Tibetan Buddhism. He looked around and was further amazed. All totaled, he uncovered twelve such meditation seats half concealed by the lush overgrowth.

By paying his respects at the altar of a great dormant civilization, did John assume he had plunged into — what? — the old Mayan sacred vortex magnetically drawing him to make that discovery? *The spiritual past is not dead*, he thought, *it is not even past, if at just the right moment you glance at just the right place with just the right receptivity*.

A rationalist might snort: there was no discovery, only a romantic believing what he wanted to believe. My friend Kenny Dessain points out that no written records cite the existence of Indian rock meditation seats. And even if in ancient Mayapán they were meditation seats for the Mayans, so what; they are just dumb rocks to us.

But a shaman does not think the way we do. Listening to John talk back in Crestone, I surmised that a shamanic experience — if John's Mayapán adventure qualifies as such

— turns our customary way of understanding on its head. First, *causality is reversed.* Ordinarily somebody does something, but in the Yucatán something was done to John. He had not set out, map and compass in hand, to locate those meditation seats but felt an inexplicable, irresistible gravitational pull toward them. Second, *form follows focus.* John's cut foot — like his thunderbolt experience and the rattlesnake bite — might have been shrugged off by others as a bad-luck accident, but those became significant events for John through the quality of the attention he paid them. Last, *reality is not either/or.* Our notion of common sense insists that those had to be *either* meditation seats *or* plain rocks. For John, though, what can be possibly one or the other carries the potentiality of both, with its latent underside often revealed in Sacred Passages and Vision Quests.

The ordeals of shamanic initiation are intended to erode the willful ego, to set aside a limited personal frame of reference, allowing in its stead a subtler attunement to the unspoken natural order to well up. For John, with that attunement snakebites become medicinal, thunderstorms segue into inner passageways, and his land outside Crestone turns into the nonprofit the Way of Nature, where hundreds have gone on retreats.

I finally finished reading *Of Water and the Spirit.* Here was Galaxy's and Neil Hogan's approach toward nature, writ large in Africa. For Malidoma Somé's people (the Dagara of Burkina Faso), little separated the spiritual and the natural, or even religion and daily life. "To a Dagara man or woman," Malidoma writes, "the material is just the spiritual taking on form. The secular is religion in a lower key — a rest area from the tension of religious and spiritual practice. Dwelling in the realm of the sacred is both exciting and terrifying. A little time out once in a while is in order."

Since I can no longer return the book to Bertha, should I loan it to John? Instead of reading it, he might haul me out to his land and plop me down on a meditation rock. That's what he did yesterday when I asked him a pointed question about shamanism. The rock he had me sit on had a worn, concave seat-level indention, actually quite comfortable. John said there were nearly fifty meditation rocks on his land, and he claimed that each of those enabled a slightly different kind of awareness — the whole field like a giant television set, say, where each channel (or rock) was attuned to, or tuned one in to, a slightly different state of consciousness. He asked whether in my sitting on that rock, which had the shape of a dolphin, I felt in any way restored, and oddly enough, I did. Unfortunately, I became so relaxed on that meditation rock that I forgot the brilliant question I'd been dying to ask.

8. Equanimity: Spirituality without the Religion

Out on John's land, sitting on the dolphin rock, I did feel top-notch; well, nature soothes the savage beast. Didn't last long. Soon I was back to being the beast: larking about, carefree, then comes a blow, knocked down, bouncing back. Lark, blow, down, back; again and again; over and over. Could this be everyone's normal back and forth, except....Except there is Bertha, greeting helps and harms equally, seeing nearly everything as positive. If equanimity were a religion, Bertha could be its pope (and I'd be its first reprobate convert).

In some religious orders, prospective monastics must display *ataraxia*, contentment with whatever is, before being allowed admission. Otherwise, possibilities for spiritual advancement will be limited by their likes and dislikes, as they are constantly buffeted about, ricocheting from preferring this to rejecting that. That's why equanimity or even-temperedness is considered by some its own psychological category, even perhaps its own kind of reality, because while the same sorry events continue to happen, with equanimity in the picture, they forfeit much of their power to internally wound.

Recently I ran into three different people here who had achieved something like ultimate equanimity, who during a Native American Sun Dance ceremony had borne pain without complaint and even transmogrified it into something like its opposite. In the ceremony a participant's breast is pierced on both sides, bones inserted through the piercings, rawhide attached to the bones, and from his breast he is thus suspended from a pole. The pain shooting through the participant's body is torture. Yet as those men* hang there in agonized suspension, the pain transports them into a different (mental) world and finally recedes, replaced by redemptive visions.

A cautionary warning: Don't try this at home. I planned on trying it nowhere yet wondered, Were there less torturous tricks for achieving lasting inner equilibrium? Here's how I proposed to find out. With folks I encountered who evinced an unusual even temper — no matter if they were religious or agnostic — I'd attempt to quietly explore how equanimity functioned in their lives.

Here's the question, the probe: When, and how, does the odd become all even?

❦

My first encounter came about because of a flat tire and involved someone who remained good-tempered, despite his having, given the ungodly hour, every reason to be anything but.

He, Dr. Dean, was already balancing many balls in the

---

* Those Sun Dance participants I ran into were Dan Retuta, Kofi Washington, and Sequoyah Trueblood, who was visiting Crestone.

air. He travels all over the state for his job as a naturopath, hosts a radio program, has formed a band, acts in the local theater group, raises chickens for their eggs, and purchases (name any broken-down object to repair, which meanwhile litters his yard), and then...lots more *thens*. In Crestone he is slightly controversial, but feisty controversies — such as over the town's water quality — boost his already high spirits. Such is the man from whom I rented a behemoth twenty-five-year-old Mercedes (more suitable for a Chicago pimp from the 1980s).

A few nights ago the Pimpmobile was bumping down an incredibly rough road. By the time I realized it wasn't the road but a flat tire, the tire looked as though it had been chewed up by an extraterrestrial bulldog. The car limped into a driveway, fortunately a friend's. Her solution was to not stop laughing as she took pictures of the ex-tire for posterity on her cell phone. Snatching her cell phone, I called Dr. Dean and cried, "Help!"

I hated phoning him. The day before he had to have risen at 3:30 AM to drive three hours to Pueblo, where he has a naturopathic practice, and there would have worked a double shift, after which he'd finish up paperwork. More than twenty-four hours after leaving Crestone, sans sleep, he'd drive the three hours back, arriving just about now. Instead of toiling on the Pimpmobile, Dr. Dean might have preferred some decadent, dreamy shut-eye. Some people are like that.

At that hour, though he might have enjoyed some well-earned rest, he would not have gone so far as to *prefer* it. For a man who hadn't slept in twenty-four hours, he was quite amused by the mess at hand. As he worked on the warped tire rim (which resembled a sculpture at the Guggenheim), Dr. Dean said a song would help keep him awake. I improvised an instant tire-repair classic about change your tire, change your mind.

My mind actually did change, seeing how a damned nuisance could mutate, given Dean's cheerful attitude, into a fairly good time. If he was an example of equanimity, it was simply because of his not preferring what most people in their right mind would have preferred. With his medical knowledge Dr. Dean pronounced the Pimpmobile sound enough to drive till I could get it to the POA garage the following morning.

In the Baca Property Owners Association garage, dead vehicles are born again.* The following morning it was a comfort to hang out in that unadorned concrete palace of down-to-earth competence. The mechanics were soothing in the matter-of-factness with which they took charge of the Pimpmobile. I was observing the old-fashioned integrity of workmanship, all skill and little ego, once synonymous with the best of America. These guys were not the type who'd meditate up at the Zen center, but in a way they were more Zen than Zen. They focused entirely on the task at hand, not distracted by anticipating a better elsewhere later. They found a few other things wrong with the old Mercedes, which they fixed without saying or charging anything. Those mechanics, that garage, displayed its own equanimity, though not of the lofty mountaintop sort. It was on the ground and derived

---

* A property owners association with its own garage and mechanics may sound odd, but otherwise the nearest mechanics' garage would be an hour away — not far, that is, unless your car is broken.

from doing work that was just what it is and nothing more and not minding doing it. Those mechanics had not only worked on Dr. Dean's car; they were also working on his principle. Which principle might be stated thus: for happiness, it is not necessary to pick, nor is it required to prefer.

If Dr. Dean was typically in a good mood, the next person I spent time with was also unflappable, but ornery. Paul Kloppenburg (Dutch name, Dutch man) is critical of the shortcomings of people here, yet he does nothing but good for them. For example, hardly having the surplus cash to do so, he just bought and planted three hundred trees on the lower mountainside, to prevent its arid soil from eroding.

We were taking a walk in the green woods that grow by the stream, where Paul noted the change in foliage since he was last there; he could have been every bush and tree's biographer. If the Earth belongs to those who stop and observe and then go lightly on their way, then those woods belong to Paul.

I was wrong about that, however. When we exited the woods, the person who legally owned them was furiously scribbling notes and taping them onto rocks for us, denouncing us for trespassing. She appeared a deeply disturbed person as she screamed at Paul that he was a common criminal and she would summon the police or give the woods to her brother to tear down and cover with concrete. How out of place her vicious rant was in this peaceful setting. What was that virago doing in Crestone? I could image her back in DC on the Tea Party side of the Senate, raving and railing. It was unnerving to be witness to that madwoman's tirade. But Paul, confident in himself, didn't blink an eye; it was all water off a duck's back.

Paul is a Buddhist, but his strange form of indignation is not, being part savage indignation. He is indignant, for example, about the self-serving way Buddhism is often practiced in America, about how few women in the Buddhist world attain positions of prominence, about how it took thirty-five years for the great Trungpa to chant in English rather than Tibetan. Some mistake his stridency for conceited cockiness. Yet a sense of justice — and a sense of Crestone as a community, not as it is but as it could be — supplants narcissistic self-importance in Paul. How else could you explain his driving four hours to Denver to see Michael in the hospital?

Michael was one mean town drunk, whose mission appeared to be to make as many people as possible as miserable as possible. In his last few months he sent out group emails, praising himself for how much he had done for Crestone. When Paul emailed back, "Name one thing," Michael stopped speaking to him. Yet when Michael lay in a Denver hospital dying of cancer, Paul drove up to comfort him, using up gas he could ill afford. Awaking from his morphine daze, Michael confessed to Paul all the horrible things he had done, and then, his regret released, became at peace. A few days later he died in that newfound peace, experienced when Paul accepted his outpouring. When Michael died, Paul was back in Crestone, doing *tonglen* (a visionary practice for taking on another's suffering) for this man who had never wished him well. Ego can accomplish many things, perhaps most things, but equanimity can drive to Denver and do *tonglen* for someone who acted like your enemy.

⬦

My next sortie into the subject of equilibrium came at Jack Siddall's tiny makeshift cabin (half resembling a cave in the Himalayas). I expected that with no real kitchen he might serve for lunch a can of beans, but formerly a professional cook, he had prepared an epicurean feast. Despite (surely not because of?) living in a cabin-cave, Jack is so healthy he has not seen a doctor for the past half century, using a knowledge of herbs and naturopathy to doctor himself. At age sixty-plus, Jack pedals his bike down and up the mountainside, carrying fifty pounds of groceries.

For Jack "spiritual times" and "good times" do not lodge in separate spheres, to be indulged on separate occasions. Last year we attended a retreat in Santa Fe, after which he asked mischievously, "Did you get lucky?" At retreats Jack usually gets lucky, young women all but swooning at his combination of dharma devotion and high spirits. They fly into Colorado to temporarily cohabit that cabin — knowing his commitment to spiritual practice will preclude setting up house with them. If you meditate *a lot*, supposedly a semiblissful repose becomes your default mental state, and so by choice Jack is in solitary retreat most of the year. His quarters may be cramped, but outside — no other building in sight, only endless valley and tall mountains — his "front yard" is space itself. Jack outspreads his arms into that space, against a bluesky backdrop, and asks, "Why have anything else?"

On a sunny, warm day like today, even I can be a take-it-easy loose goose, let come what may. But what happens when come-what-may is the person you most love dying? Earlier in the year Jack spent two months in Montana, where that person was his mother. He maneuvered her bed down the stairs into the living room, where she was surrounded by eight of her eleven children. Earlier, while Mrs. Siddall could still get about, Jack took her on a Centering Prayer retreat with Father Thomas Keating, and afterward she said that it was the best experience of her life. "Better than having eleven children?" Jack teased her. "Yes," she said, "better." One would expect her last months of painful decline to be a rain of tears and tearful farewells. But Jack did not assume that that tear-fulfilling prophecy was how it had to be. He knew only that he needed to be there. Despite the all-too-real sadness, the closeness and warmth with her and with his family was a solace unlike anything Jack or his siblings had ever experienced.

My last study is a handyman who looks like one, with his lean body, often dressed in splotchy shirt and paint-spattered jeans. Howie Ostler talks like a philosopher, though — his compact frame barely containing the enthusiasm — as he expounds on rarified topics. Looks like a handyman, talks like a metaphysician, but acts like a holy fool? For his skilled repairs he lets his client pay him whatever they want, claiming his pleasure is the work itself, and if forced to name a fee, Howie will name one so ridiculously low that the client barters to get it higher.

His chief peculiarity, though, concerns pain. It goes back to when he was sixteen and probably the sole Mormon youth in Utah secretly studying hypnosis (from mail-order brochures). At the dentist's office for a painful extraction, young Howie opted for self-hypnosis rather than a numbing agent. "No, no," the dentist dismissed such nonsense. "Son, that is one bad idea." Seeing that the stubborn boy was not going to yield, the dentist reluctantly relented, though he kept a hypodermic of anesthetic nearby. Howie concentrated solely on his breath (just as the hypnosis brochures taught). Was there pain? If so, he didn't feel it, his attention focused single-pointedly elsewhere. He has never required an anesthetic for medical procedures since then.

Yet Howie is no stranger to the slings and arrows of a body pierced with hurt. Once he went for days — days that stretched out like weeks — suffering a practically unbearable toothache. Working as a handyman, he has gotten debris stuck in his eye, more excruciating yet. However, after a few days he would remember to withdraw concentration from the pain by witnessing himself witnessing it. When he did so, the suffering no longer exercised veto power over any chance for a good mood.

In lists of opposites (short/tall, north/south, etc.), pleasure is invariably set in the opposite column across from pain. Howie knows only too well the difference, but since awareness — neutral, pure consciousness — flows through both, he tunes in to the awareness and affably accepts both, not exulting in one or bemoaning the other. He may now be a handyman by profession, but when it comes to equanimity, he's a grand pooh-bah.

One definition of unhappiness is receiving what you don't want. What, I wonder, do most people I know not want most? Clinical depression, maybe. Yet I also know people prone to depression who are not undone by it. Neil Hogan the Buddhist "nonshamanic shaman," for example, is hardly immune to melancholy's darker moods. Some years ago depression sat on him, like a black bear twiddling its claws. His sole comfort at that time came from living outdoors, sleeping in a tent on the earth, as winter shivered in its own dark mood. At dawn he lit the small camp stove just long enough to unfreeze his limbs sufficiently to insert them into stiff jean legs and shirt sleeves. He did not rush to take Prozac, though, or make an appointment with a therapist or listen to self-help tapes. He did not become sad(der) because he was sad. Neil knew what he had to do.

Which was nothing. Neil's version of doing nothing — his not rushing off to a therapist, his not being depressed about being depressed — may have indicated an imperturbability in his heart's otherwise heaviness. H_2O remains H_2O, in the sense that it remains chemically equanimous, through its mutations through water, steam, and ice. In their balanced steady state maintained despite and through moods, fellow sufferers like Neil may exhibit the human equivalent of underlying "H_2O-ness."

For the people described here, their grace under pressure did not require church or prayers or spiritual stoicism. In the suffering itself, Sun Dancers like Dan and Kofi found its antidote, as did the sixteen-year-old Howie when the pangs from the dentist's drill dissolved in a field of awareness. Others attain such evenness simply by wearing daily pressures lightly (Dr. Dean), or by shedding the thin skin of ego-defensiveness (Paul Kloppenburg), or not getting caught up in expectations (Jack Siddall). Beyond them, there is probably in Crestone one true master of equanimity — if anyone is — and I determined to draw him out on its even-stephen wonders.

Since his job confronts him with joy and sorrow daily, I questioned Tsoknyi Rinpoche: "Rinpoche, I have read that suffering and happiness can ultimately be experienced as similar or even as one. Can that possibly be so?" What answer could he give? A flat *no* would deny the basic Buddhist goal of transforming negativity into *bodhicitta* (a mind of understanding, happiness, and compassion). A flat *yes* would invite incredulity and, worse, hint that he among mortals has achieved this feat. Tsoknyi's modest response left the door open, though, to what now seems unimaginable but one day may not be. "I have tasted it," he said. "But I'm not there yet."

I am light-years from "there," but through the folks in this chapter — some professedly spiritual, others not — I have had a faint taste of equanimity, vicariously. Though tasteless, it tastes good.

9. The Mind Electric

1

Suppose you awoke one fine morning to find all your problems gone — gone, mysteriously gone. Not only was there nothing to worry about, but it seemed there was not even the possibility of worry. Outside it looked an ordinary day, as familiar as an old spoon, but today the spoon shone with a strange, indefinable luster. The morning was clear, fresh after last night's rain, with the promise of more sunny days to come. Such is the image of a spontaneous awakening that Eckhart Tolle popularized in *The Power of Now*, where he fell asleep suicidal and woke up into a morning glowing with perfection. Yet despite a Facebook page on spontaneous awakenings and the popular Adyashanti teaching it on the internet, evidently it may be as rare as winning the lottery, and a lottery for which you cannot buy tickets.

If spontaneous awakenings occur so relatively seldom, why not simply dismiss them as a curious but insignificant fluke of the mind (comparable to the Japanese man who memorized pi to the 87,000th digit)? Why not? Because, just conceivably, they may supply a foretaste of what elusive fabled enlightenment, or ultimate human well-being, is like. The few people in Crestone who have experienced such a so-called awakening afterward reported that worry and obsession dropped away like a snake shedding its skin, and that life's gloomy downside had less Velcro to attach to.

What does a spontaneous awakening look, feel, taste like? Let's examine Ralph Abram's sudden influx of clarity and wonder, which happened long ago and far away but that would eventually lead him to Crestone. Let's time-travel for a moment back to then.

For the price of a cheap air ticket in the late 1960s you could arrive overnight at some exotic or romantic destination like, say, Greece. There by blue Aegean waters you confided to strangers / new friends where your daring journey would next lead you. Except for Ralph, that is, who had been arrested for smoking marijuana and locked in a Greek jail. The Greek prisoners glared at him and muttered in an incomprehensible tongue what he assumed were threats that boded him no good. He dreaded to nod off asleep.

Somehow he slept. The next morning he awoke — could it be the same jail? Were these the same prisoners? It felt as though...as though he'd never truly been awake before. His cellmates, who yesterday had loomed like Mediterranean thugs, this morning seemed his brothers, wishing him only well. The light streaming through the window, well, if love were visible, it might shine like this and caress you as softly. A spontaneous awakening like Ralph's usually happens only after one is boxed into an impossible corner. But after that morning even prison turned out to be not such a bad place to be.

Two years later, out of jail and back in America, Ralph discovered that he possessed unexpected abilities. He could enter into violent situations and calm them, and he could intuit what was troubling others and comfort them. He started a commune because he assumed that anyone could have this blissful understanding and that was what everyone wanted. To sustain itself financially, the commune smuggled in marijuana from Mexico, yet even when Ralph was arrested and served prison time again, it did not interrupt his mind at ease. In prison he taught yoga, fasted with the Berrigan brothers to protest the Vietnam War, and befriended the toughest inmates. Whether he was inside prison or out did not matter; it seemed nothing could go seriously wrong again.

Until it did. His temporary enlightenment ended as abruptly as it had begun. After his parole, Ralph was sauntering along in New York City, not a care in the world, when a sickly green condensation of air materialized. The condensation, or projection or whatever it was (a "succubus" he now metaphorically calls it), seeped into him, or at least it felt that way. And, just like that, he was ordinary again — ordinary, at loose ends, and often irritable. After an experience like his ends, the few who have experienced it may spend the rest of their life searching for its sequel or equal. Ralph bought an Airstream trailer to give him mobility in the search.

He drove the Airstream out West by Southwest, where he decided to visit all the Buddhist stupas. It proved a long, tiring drive to Crestone, and once he was there it required only a glance to realize it hadn't been worth it. Nobody was on the street except a three-legged dog. But then Ralph met Mark Jacobi and liked him, and if somebody like Mark lived here, here must be all right. And so began *la vita nova*, in which he would become mayor of the town and afterward start Crestone Telecom, in his efforts to begin again after a spontaneous awakening ends.

❧

Besides Ralph, a few others in Crestone have had similar experiences, when the misbehaving psyche suddenly is on its best behavior. Perfection, at least for a while, became the norm. *Perfection* is an ideal that is usually found only in the religious sphere, when your sins are washed clean and you are robed in redemption. For these Crestonians, however, the sudden electric rightness of everything transpired in circumstances quite mundane.

Of the spontaneous awakenings I've heard of, handyman Howie Ostler's was unique in not being cooked up in a pressure cooker of misery. For weeks he had been feeling increasingly well, physically and emotionally. This was back in the early 1970s, when speculation about enlightenment was in the air. While he was driving down a back road, George Harrison's "My Sweet Lord" was lilting from the car radio. Howie pulled off the side of the road to puzzle out what in our own lives, if anything, the song corresponded to. He determined not to budge from the spot until — well, *until*.

Howie tried to concentrate but would get distracted by, say, planning something yummy for dinner. Some psycho-physiological mechanism inside us, he concluded, does not want to be enlightened. For survival the human ego may have evolved to consider everything primarily in relation to its own needs. (For seeing reality, uncolored by projections, a dog or cat may well be more enlightened than a person.) But after he had spent some hours meditating by the side of the road, Howie's interior monologue ran out of things to say. He forgot to question what "my sweet Lord" represented; instead of a stream of free associations, there was only pure awareness in which thoughts rose up and faded away without tarnishing it. In most religious traditions, peel away enough layers of the persona and you come to an indestructible kernel of selfhood, often called the "soul." For Howie it seemed that his surface personality had peeled away, but what was left was something as boundless and intangible as consciousness itself. Everything seemed right just as it was, and Howie could see no reason to return to his former life, with its duties and responsibilities. But there was also no reason not to, so he climbed back into his car and drove merrily home.

After his roadside realization Howie's mood state for the next fortnight was one of unbroken elation. At first he avoided using the word *I*, for there seemed nothing, no homunculus inside, to which it corresponded. But not to use the first-person pronoun to refer to who was standing where he was standing proved too cumbersome, and *I* stole back into his conversation. But whether as "I" or "not I," from morning to night he was continuously joyful. His wife suspected that if he was that happy, he must be having an affair and threatened to divorce him. Had that intense ecstasy blazed much longer, Howie thought, his internal circuits would have shorted and fried. Now thirty years later what trace, if any, of that mental breakthrough is still evident?

Maybe only one. That wordless roadside epiphany may faintly linger on in how his moods do not fluctuate ceaselessly, one moment up, the next moment down. Howie used to play the card game Hearts on the computer, becoming excited if he was winning and excited in a different way if he was losing. Till he thought, *I want to be a gambler — not just in cards but in work and also romantic relations — who does not gamble away his tranquility, who is not one person when losing and another person when winning.* Recently I overheard him say to his friend Vivia, "I've discovered the way not to gamble in love. Simply don't expect anything in return." "And how do you do that," Vivia laughed as she answered her own question. "By not having sex?"

Howie wonders what would happen to his good spirits were he to forfeit the abundant comforts that now cushion him. But most people, if compelled to live the way he does — hard work, no home of his own, few possessions — would not call it luxury but would whine about life's unfairness.

Though Howie once earned handsomely, we have already seen how now as a handyman when potential clients ask his fee, he lets them name whatever they want to pay. Pattison Kane recently came up to him reporting, "My new landlady just loves you, Howie. You keep her place flawless and never charge her anything." I overheard him haggling with my neighbor Molly that year* about the price of his fix-

---

* Practically every year I had to find a new habitat to rent, sublet, or house-sit — the unknown of it adding a slightly spicy flavor to the excitement each time of coming to Crestone.

ing her car. It was an odd haggling, with him wanting less and her bargaining for him to take more.

During that lightning bolt of insight now years ago, he awoke from the dream of material good into a lighter and airier dream, in which he doesn't need to possess to appreciate. He finds the act of awareness more exciting than any particular thing it can be aware of wanting. His pleasures are those associated with youth — action and the difficult challenge and spontaneous adventure — rather than those with age, like security and the comfortable and the familiar. Three or four decades after his spontaneous awakening, Howie Ostler retains many traits of a boy, a boy who has had an unusual experience.

Howie's short-lived spontaneous awakening, occurring when he was already in good spirits, did not ignite a full night-to-day transformation as Ralph's in the Greek jail had. Zoe de Bray's experience more resembled Ralph's, rewriting her character in an instant. (And like Ralph's, its aftermath would eventually lead to Crestone.)

Zoe, born in 1947, grew up in favored circumstances, outwardly. In their Pennsylvania town, her father was the prosperous Yale-educated eye surgeon, a respected pillar of the community. At home, however, he was alcoholic and out of control, and his idea for his daughters' future omitted college: make babies, not careers. As soon as she was old enough, Zoe escaped to New York City, practically penniless, where from a public phone booth she dialed one magazine publisher after another. *House Beautiful*, which she confused with *Harper's Bazaar*, asked her in for an interview and hired her on the spot. Zoe's wildest hopes turned into reality in the neon city: eventually she worked for NBC and started a literary magazine and starred in an off-Broadway play. However, on the side she was taking recreational drugs, nothing, though, compared to the amount of alcohol she was consuming, and, well, one thing led to another. Such as living on the streets. At that desperate low point, she found a dime and made a phone call: this time to Alcoholics Anonymous.

Zoe must have sounded dire indeed, for the woman from AA interrupted her tale of woe: "Don't move! Stay right there. I'll be there in fifteen minutes. No, ten." She picked up Zoe and drove straight to a hospital. As Zoe entered the glare of the hospital's entryway, something snapped inwardly — as when you bolt upright out of a bad dream. The brightness of the bald fluorescent lighting dimmed next to the explosion of light in her mind. It felt as though her personal awareness had broken free of its limitations and become part of consciousness per se.

That moment of sudden lucidity lengthened into months, months vibrant and inexplicably happy. For a woman who had once suffered emotional deprivation, Zoe now felt connection everywhere. If a car drove past, say, she felt inwardly its revving force and metallic intensity; if she noticed a cat, a feline sinuousness slithered within her. The unshakable burdens long weighing her down sloughed off on their own. She did not struggle to give up alcohol; from one moment to the next it lost its addictive appeal. (Zoe's mother, a far "stronger" woman, could never give up drinking, believing life would be unbearable without it.) After her release from the hospital Zoe accidentally strayed into a bad neighborhood, frightened at being lost, but then experienced such a feeling of being at home in herself she thought, *To be really and truly lost — that's impossible.*

Spontaneous awakenings do not last forever. Ralph's continued for seven years, while Howie Ostler's, in its intensity, for only a fortnight. Zoe's continued for several months, months of grace, in which each dawn rose like the world's first morning and around every corner awaited another wonder. After such exaltation, what follows? Zoe would go on to college, get her BA, her PhD, do postdoctoral work in Germany, master Sanskrit, get married (and reluctantly divorced), move to Crestone, and start a spiritual group here (affiliated with the 17th Karmapa). When those high-octane months of pitch-perfect excitements finally exhausted themselves, Zoe did not regret her reimmersion into the "ordinary." For the ordinary was where the knots of her upbringing, now less foreboding, could at last be loosened.

She returned to the ordinary, but with a difference. After her awakening Zoe was drawn to meditation. And meditate she did. Tallying it up, she spent more than ten years in solitary retreat, familiarizing herself with the mind's ways of acting and reacting. Now at ease in her own skin, Zoe hoped to accomplish the unthinkable — forgiving her father. With her perspective widened, the scale of his abuse now seemed small, and she found empathy for him, the way one might for an angry, hurt child. Besides, she was no angel herself. Again and again she discovered that if she remained quiet and receptive, that for any problem her flux of impressions settled on their own into a surprising, suggestive solution.

Although spontaneous awakening is likened to temporary enlightenment, Zoe found it did not melt obstacles into air or that she no longer knew human woes. Problems usually carried less weight, though; anger had a shorter half-life; thoughts of the future wore a sly Mona Lisa–like smile. Unlike in those dark days when everything seemed over, done, and finished, she now suspects that even enlightenment is not the end of the story.

What moral, if moral there be, do these before-and-after stories of awakening suggest? Perhaps three. (1) Before, Zoe could not shake off unwilled and unwanted habitual behaviors (alcoholism, father-hatred); after, they practically evaporated on their own, suggesting: *We are not our habits.* (2) Before, like the good Mormon youth he was, Howie dreamed of the communal good and of raising a family and achieving financial success; after, he became an independent thinker and divorced bachelor and entirely nonmaterialistic, suggesting: *We are not our past.* (3) The night Ralph landed in prison he felt that his life was as good (i.e., as bad) as done; after, the next morning, he awoke in his cell into unprecedented well-being, suggesting: *We are not even necessarily our present situations.*

Might make you wish you could have a spontaneous awakening, too.

Yes, suppose you wanted a spontaneous awakening but were clueless as to how to make it happen — what then?

In his big retreat tent on the mountainside outside Crestone, Tsoknyi Rinpoche instructs his students in a most unusual topic: how to tap into the nature of their minds, how, beyond its ever-changing contents, to experience consciousness itself directly. The simple exercise he teaches requires only a few minutes, but often retreatants report that for those minutes they had (or so it felt) a sort of spontaneous awakening, possibly a little foretaste of enlightenment.

Here — to the limited extent it can be conveyed in print — is how it goes. Tsoknyi has them sit alert, posture upright but relaxed. Then they raise their arms, and like boulders hurled down a ravine, their hands crash down loudly against their thighs. Simultaneously they let out an ear-splitting, mind-shattering sound that stops thought dead in its tracks. After being thus stunned into the present moment, instead of listening to more teachings, they silently linger in thought-free clarity with no object of focus. They are existing for those moments in unadorned, unproblematic, unboundaried pure consciousness. If an unnecessary idea begins to form, it's like a train they are about to board but then don't. (They have, for those moments, joined the fraternity of Ralph and Howie and Zoe.)

This lucid, empty-of-content state is agreeable but feels hardly more extraordinary than the relief of, say, putting down a heavy rucksack one has shouldered for too long. Or, to use a different metaphor, as though a faint but grating noise in the distance has subsided, leaving in its place soothing quiet. For that moment — and it may last no longer — burdens and worries, having no mind support, cease to exist. There is no past, there is no future, and there's not even a present (or nothing demanding their immediate attention), yet they are still here and pleased to be here. Absence of thought leaves no sense of absence; oddly it creates an unfamiliar, albeit pleasant, heightened sense of presence.

A strange relief it is, not to have to be the hero (or anything else) of their own lives. That life they left behind for the retreat week, of home and family and work, may boast nearly every object and event conceivable, yet not this blue sky–like absence-presence. They had climbed a fraction of the way up a mountainside outside Crestone not for something tangible, it turns out, but for a taste of spontaneous awakening, so to speak, an hors d'oeuvre of enlightenment.

II

Tsoknyi's silent retreats in Crestone end with an informal get-together at the Desert Sage restaurant, and rarely have folks been so keen to talk, chattering madly away. First of all, they have something to talk about; it's spilling out of them, their having eschewed human verbosity for a week. They discuss whether or not Tsoknyi was in top form; they meet their hitherto mute neighbors; everyone says what they gained (or failed to) from the retreat.

"What did it feel like for you," one person asks, "to go from thoughts to thought-free awareness?" At that table they improvise a little game of inventing up-to-date metaphors for when the mind is suddenly unburdened of its endless, exhausting inner monologue. One woman proposed, for example, "It's the difference between a GPS's step-by-step vocal instructions and knowing the route by heart."

What might be more helpful than a new metaphor, however, would be someone who could illustrate how awareness itself, and not thought-chatter, can navigate the turns and traffic of daily life.

꙳

If anyone could show us what the mind uncolored by its transient thoughts is like, it may be, ironically, the man who has the most to think about. Tsoknyi Rinpoche has set up house in the eye of the storm: every few minutes present him with something else pressing to attend to, from supporting his nunneries in Tibet to establishing schools in Nepal to creating dharma websites, to traveling the world giving teachings, to attending to his thousands of students' welfare. Not to be consumed day and night with thoughts, plans, concerns, arrangements, and problem-solving might seem a sheer impossibility.

At Tsoknyi's last Crestone retreat someone asked, "Can I drive a car while in a thought-free state of mind?" "Let me say no," Tsoknyi replied jovially. "I don't want you suing me when you're in an accident." Yet when privately I asked him for a personal vignette of thought-free action, his example was driving in traffic, not just any traffic but the bumper-car lunacy of Kathmandu. He was there supervising the translation of an entire Buddhist lineage, but after getting to his office through a world-class traffic gnarl he needed not a lineage of texts but a case of liniment. But after a while he tried driving without a tiresome mental commentary about this insane congestion or that crazy driver, and though the commute took longer, there were no accidents, no poles run into, no turns down wrong streets. Evidently when thoughts are not in the driver's seat, awareness still can be.

Tsoknyi apparently can attend to his thoughts for the moment(s) necessary and then dispatch them with effortless ease. Once over some urgent matter Esteban Hollander, who runs Tsoknyi's organization in Crestone, needed to contact him in Nepal. Tsoknyi answered his cell phone on the first ring. Courteous as ever, Esteban inquired whether this was a convenient time for him to talk. "A perfect moment," Tsoknyi said. They conducted their business over the phone; Tsoknyi was wholly there with him. However, Esteban kept hearing noise in the background and finally asked what it was. "Oh, that," Tsoknyi answered. "I'm in the midst of giving this elaborate teaching for a few hundred people but they are chanting right now, so…" His mind had shifted from that esoteric teaching to the practical business at hand without his consciousness changing at all.

One advantage of a clear, uncluttered state of mind is that when you reach your destination, whether a tiny office in Kathmandu or halfway round the globe, you are less fatigued by the journey. Tsoknyi is rarely exhausted. On a book promotion tour in 2012 he traveled three months nonstop. For three months, there was every day a different city, every day more interviews, every night another reading. Accompanying him, Esteban was ready to drop and, though not complaining (Esteban doesn't), pined for home sweet home. Tsoknyi, to the contrary, remained unburdened and untroubled, fresh. He never sighed for home (the past); he was unconcerned about whether the next night's reading (the future) would draw three hundred or three; and if in the present his thoughts took a troublesome turn, well, he knew how to handle thoughts. He arrived back in Crestone looking as relaxed as though he'd spent those months on vacation.

And once back in Crestone, Tsoknyi proceeded to teach the way to peace and mental freedom, not through particular spiritual beliefs but through using no belief-thoughts at all. And outside the tent hardly a sound stirred, just the landscape's vastness and spaciousness silently illustrating what was with difficulty being said inside.

10. When There Is Here and Bitter Is Sweet

Imagining perhaps a spiritual Land of Oz, tourists occasionally come to inspect the curiosity of Crestone. Yet with the religious centers tucked away on the mountainside and with the "downtown's" budget Western set, they find little to inspect. "Where is it? Where is it?" they demand. Kizzen Laki, the newspaper editor, laughs, "Oh, Crestone doesn't exist on the physical plane."

Is there anything about Crestone worth a trip (providing once here you could find it)? Most of what happens here is quite ordinary. ("Crestone is a drinking town," so goes one witticism, "with a spiritual problem.") When Mark Elliott received and, short of cash, declined Sam Moves Camp's invitation to the Lakota Reservation, that was an ordinary exchange between one person and another. But when Mark dreamed of the reservation and then later the actual reservation matched the dream's image — really, what is one to make of that?

There is a word, however, for the bizarre intuition embodied in Mark's dream. *Nonduality* implies that the distances or dissimilarities between here and there, or between you and me, may conceal hidden affinities, like siblings who have lost track of each other.* In a further philosophical sense, it holds that we are all of one essence, all drops from the same ocean, which answers Einstein's final question — "Is the universe friendly?" — with a resounding *yes!* More than friendly, the universe is family; more than family, it and us are seamlessly joined. As esoteric as the word is, *nonduality* may not be all that uncommon. Romantic swains used to sigh that one love flowed through the two bodies. Most religions propagate some form of nonduality, such as Christianity's Father, Son, and Holy Spirit betraying the same essence. A Zen teacher will hold up a finger and a thumb of one hand and ask, "Is this one or two?"

For all its unlikelihood, nonduality may be an idea whose time has come. Dividing a small, ravaged planet into us and them, which then slips into us *versus* them, which can further slide into us destroying them (or worse, vice versa), may not furnish the most helpful political model today. To see the other as not unlike oneself might be crucial for a boat navigating the treacherous straits between feuding ethnicities and hostile nationalities with seven and a half billion passengers aboard.

❧

In Crestone resides probably the only person writing a PhD dissertation on nonduality as a means to solving global problems. Its PhD-candidate author is easy to recognize here: she

---

* A nonhuman example of nonduality would be migrating flocks of birds that harmonize their flight patterns through an awareness that resides in each individual bird but transcends it at the same time.

is Japanese, sports a Beatles mophead haircut, and appears to be about twenty-five (twenty-four years younger than her actual age).

Megumi Sugihara first heard the word *nonduality* when a housemate was listening to the popular spiritual teacher Adyashanti on the radio. At a fundamental level, Adyashanti said, we are all interconnected, essentially one essence. Meg thought, *What nonsense*, since at the most fundamental level she had no trouble distinguishing herself from everybody else. To realize nonduality, Adyashanti went on, do not identify with your thoughts. *How ridiculous*, Meg silently retorted: in academia the name of the game was identifying with and staking claims to your ideas.

Still, her curiosity pricked, she began enacting small experiments on the sly. In a public place she fixated on a weird character in an outlandish getup who irritated her. Then she posed the question, *What if that person and I are linked together in some strange but unknowable necessity?* Imagining that secret collusion, her irritation at the weirdo slowly subsided. Performing such experiments in nondualistic empathy — even if they were only a helpful fiction — infused in her a faint sense of belonging to a larger whole. Whether nonduality was more than a fiction, she could not say, for hers were thought-exercises in nonduality, not a genuine experience of it.

But then Megumi experienced the real thing. In 2004 she attended a leadership conference held in Crestone, and... well, guess what happened. She met John Milton, and before she could think twice she was embarked on a wilderness retreat. After a few days in the wilds, inner and outer seemed no longer segregated. The trees near her campsite seemed intimately implicated in her sense of being. When she looked steadily at a particular tree, without any commentary, she felt it growing psychologically in her, kindred to the way it grew physically outside her. The tree, the act of observation, and the person observing — gradually it blurred, in the happiest way, where one left off and the other began. Could other this-versus-that scenarios be likewise bridged or other distances equally spanned? Meg decided to stay in Crestone for two years and write her dissertation on nondual approaches to sociopolitical problem-solving (those two years have by now extended into eight).

A slight hitch was the question, Are there any examples of nonduality in politics? Maybe one: Gandhi. Gandhi said he was not fighting for Indian independence *against* the English; rather he was fighting (though he did not like the word *fighting*) *for* both Indians *and* the British, to liberate the latter from their self-destructive colonial mentality. Meg's case study was not Gandhi, however, but a more manageable example: John Milton. Not only does John teach nonduality, but some of his students put it into practice, like the executive who instituted "nondual" policies such as workers' rights and sustainability at Nike.

To illustrate nonduality, her dissertation might have included someone else besides John. Herself. Her learning to re-see in nondual terms began when she conceived of herself and the weirdo as parts of a larger whole, and at an anti-nuclear demonstration when she imagined her opponents as blurred images of herself in a distorted mirror. Were that the case, she puzzled, what might she say to them? Perhaps, simply, "Couldn't we, without giving up our positions, be less hostile and show more empathy to one another?" Meg dismissed her efforts as inconsequential, artificial experiments, yet in method acting one assumes an artificial emotion and feels it till it becomes a real one. Her dissertation was Meg's version of method-acting nonduality.

❧

Yet even supposing you could do it, what practical benefit could issue from practicing nonduality? Megumi's teacher, John Milton, used mind-body nondualistic healing to save himself from lying in a hospital bed semi-indefinitely. A few years ago, as we saw, that's where John was, in poststroke condition, helpless and (according to the doctors) hopeless, unable to move his corpse-like limbs. With his mind John guided his energy — through "inner tai chi" — to frozen parts of his inert body, and after a month, thanks to the nonduality of body and mind, walked out of the hospital, to the doctors' amazement.

As we schmoozed in the Bliss Café John related an earlier instance of nondualistic mind-body healing, which took place when he was working in remote Nepal. One evening a coworker said, "Care to go look at the rhinoceroses?" That was an offer no one could refuse, especially with no other diversions around. They were not gone long, however, before John realized his coworker was drunk, driving recklessly through a sal forest. They barely dodged trees, until they didn't and one branch smacked John directly in his left eye.

The pain was excruciating, and with his left eye John could see nothing, could not make out a single form. The pain was too severe to permit an eight- to ten-day trek to the nearest medical facility. What to do? Having long practiced qigong, John began funneling chi (energy) into his palm and pressing his palm over his eye. After a couple of weeks the curtain of blackness pulled back slightly, and each day it receded a little further, until he regained entire vision in that eye. (He did not, however, focus any chi on his unwounded right eye, and that eye is much weaker today.)

Thus John learned that an active mind and an inert body are not one (the same), but neither are they many (separate, unrelated). A blinded eye and a warmed palm are not one, but neither are they many. Benefiting from that paradox inspired John to teach his students, like Meg, a form of nonduality that overrides barriers between mind and body and between self and nature.

Postreligious Nonduality

Nonduality (which has many other names) forms the basis of much religious morality, as when we are instructed to treat the other/neighbor/stranger/enemy as we would have ourselves treated. There is another form, a postreligious form, of nonduality, however, that has allowed one man now living in Crestone to penetrate some of the world's worst hells, from dungeons in Morocco to genocide in Rwanda, and to ameliorate them. In his version, opposites — good and bad, heights and abysses, clarity and obscurity, progress and impediments — retain their separate, opposed character (no blurring of identities here) but also have the potential to collaborate in an unimaginable redeeming whole.

Before coming to Crestone James O'Dea was in a position

to save condemned lives, secure political prisoners' release, and get victims spared tortures, when he was director of Amnesty International in Washington. His day's agenda might mean confronting genocide, torture, rape, ethnic cleansing, concentration camps, and the innocently condemned — the horrors of an era crowded into a single morning. When seven innocent men in Yemen were to be executed, for example, James persuaded the Yemeni ambassador to intervene, and those seven men are alive today. The King's Prison, hidden deep within Morocco's Atlas Mountains, was infamous for starving and torturing prisoners, and whoever disappeared behind its walls disappeared forever. James denounced the King's Prison in a speech before the US Congress, and the next day the prison closed.* If his job at Amnesty brought him face-to-face with the unspeakable, retaining his sanity while dealing with it necessitated finding some saving grace amid the ashes or (in the medieval mystic's phrase) discovering "the garden among the flames." Despite being both a mystic and an activist, James was hardly prepared to discover, as later he would, time and again, that the very best that human beings are capable of often arose on the spot where the worst atrocities had been committed.

In Rwanda James watched as a mother forgave the murderers of her son. In Israel a family whose teenage daughter had been killed by Palestinian terrorists desired retribution, until they read their daughter's last diary entry: "I dream of

---

* One man, starved in that prison for sixteen years, upon his release flew to Washington to thank James in person. James took him to a nearby Mexican restaurant and asked, "What would you like? There's tacos, there's fajitas, there's —" The man interrupted, "It's food!"

peace with the Palestinians." Instead of revenge, they formed the Bereaved Family Forum, to bring together Israeli and Palestinian parents whose children had died violently, to know and comfort one another. At such moments James could almost feel he was witnessing the birth of a new humanity, one unyoked from the old vengeful eye-for-an-eye violence that has dominated human history.

Picture those old-fashioned clocks where the pendulum would arc far right, then far left, back and forth, and only by vacillating between opposite directions could it fulfill its function of telling the time. A similar vacillation, James feels, may animate our lives. The ground of our existence may not be goodness, as optimists affirm, or evil, as pessimists suspect, but a good-bad interplay that can at times take us deeper and beyond either. James quotes the Sufi proverb: "Your heart cannot say *yes* until the sweet becomes bitter and the bitter becomes sweet." That *yes* may be the ultimate nonduality, and James would realize the bittersweetness it entails as never before after he came to Crestone. But before Crestone...

Before Crestone: A Sufi tale. As he reached young manhood, James decided that England (to where he had moved from his native Ireland) was nice, very nice indeed, but *nice* needed counterbalancing with *wild.** He thus went to teach in Turkey,

---

* A certain contrariness forms a leitmotif in James's life, from childhood on. Around age eleven he insisted on joining a monastery; a couple of years later he robbed the monastery bursar and went on the lam; the next year, after publicly drawing attention to England's neglected aged, he was named "Teenager of the Year" in London.

despite its unremitting civil violence (circa 1978–1980), where he would be knifed in the street and his house machine-gunned. Yet simultaneously began his encounters with an Arabian Nights sequence of Sufi masters.

In Istanbul James frequented an antiquarian bookstore where old men hovered by the stove in the back, while only occasionally did a stray customer wander in. Unbeknownst to him, the old men were Sufi masters, and the bookstore owner was Sheikh Mahmud Efendi himself, a legend in Sufi circles. Sheikh Mahmud grew fond of his English customer and advised, "Mr. James, study Islam. Above all, study Islam." Despite that advice, and fond as Sheikh Mahmud might be of him, James realized that the sheikh would never initiate him into Islam's secret fraternities and mysteries. The sheikh's introduction to Islam opened for James a new spiritual door; his refusal to initiate James, though, appeared the next moment to slam it shut.

Then a stranger on the street handed James a page hastily jotted on and torn from a notebook, which contained only a telephone number. Intrigued, James called the number, and an old man answered who identified himself as Hasan Shushud (if known outside Turkey it's as the author of *Masters of Wisdom of Central Asia*). When James arrived for their meeting, Shushud greeted him, "Now I will introduce you to a great master." The great master was tea. As they sat drinking it, Shushud told him he could forget Islam and, as for that, Christianity, too. All that was necessary was for James to pray and fast and meditate. (In fact, praying and meditating and fasting were what Native Americans once made pilgrimages to Crestone to do.)

How peculiar, James thought, as he kept meeting holy men

one after another, where the latest one's counsel invariably contradicted the preceding one's. One would instruct him to observe rituals; the next, to pay no attention to outward forms. One cajoled him that Islam was the sole gate to Truth; the next, that Islam possessed no special door to realization. Almost uncanny: whatever one of them said, which sounded profound at the time, the next would say the opposite, which sounded even more profound, until.... Finally all the advice, all the paths, canceled each other out, and without the support of a particular tradition but also without its limitations, he stood philosophically naked in the world.

And possibly that was the point. The Sufi Metin Bobaroglu admonished James explicitly, "You are in grave danger of becoming an ordinary saint. You must stop all manner of religious practice. Do not even think of God." Metin concluded, "You are a page scribbled all over that needs to become blank and full of space." The dualities that characterize religious life — immanence versus transcendence, sacred versus secular, Christianity versus Islam — in effect erased each other, leaving...that's what he would later come to Crestone to find out, what on Metin's blank page might be inscribed, after all the scribbling was erased.

In Greek Orthodoxy any statement about holiness must fulfill two criteria: (1) it must be paradoxical because no neat, coherent human thought can contain God and (2) it must be apophatic, that is, it must lead into silent awe, because the sacred overflows formulations about sacredness. The Sufi masters, by contradicting one another at every point, had gone far on extricating James from the enchantment of forms and formulations, leaving a blank page or rather a heart opened to a larger nameless receptivity. On leaving Turkey, James thought, *Not bad for a thirty-two-year-old*, his age then. This disidentification from forms would serve him well, when James went to work for Amnesty International, in worlds (forms) going up in flames.

⟨⟨⟩

Possibly James imbibed enough of those Sufi masters' outlook that its geographical corollary could be found only somewhere somewhat nondualistic, that is, whose social and physical pluses and minuses, even while contradictory, completed each other. Thus, when he was looking for a new place to live conducive to his being both a mystic and an activist, Crestone lured him by being harsh of terrain but spiritual of outlook, by offering a cohesive human community but one dominated by its beyond-human natural surroundings. Anyone moving to Crestone should be prepared for the bitter: winter with days below minus 10 and 15 degrees, spring with its plague of mosquitoes, summer with is blinding dust storms. These trials or inconveniences combined for James with the sweetness of Crestone: all the remarkable men and women here who had escaped "the labyrinth of seduction," as he calls the traps of materialistic culture, and instead attempt to harmonize themselves with the environment.

When his sons now visit him, they go mountain climbing and delight in Crestone's beauty. James values more the other side: its rude austerity. The harsh seasons, the default solitude, the absence of distractions are all an incitement to stay inside and put his inner house in order. He needed the hardship and solitude to stop, to confront the unfinished business within himself, so that — unlike in the troubled, blighted zones where he has worked — the unexamined emotional turmoil would not become a dark inheritance, unconsciously passed on from generation to generation.

And just possibly he might do as much good in Crestone, but a different kind of good, as he did at Amnesty International. If we live in a world both obviously and subtly connected across distances, then one could work within a smaller circumference but at a deeper level, and possibly ameliorate just as much suffering. At Amnesty no sooner did James handle one problem than another catastrophe erupted. He was not just putting Band-Aids on sores — for the wounds were acute and the healing often radical — but if he did not do his job there, someone else would. James wanted now to get at the source, the societal malfunction, that underlies human misery. How to tackle the problem at the root?

The sorrow of history, James concluded, is how often victims turn into perpetuators. Those who are wounded, when their turn comes, wound others. Lenin's and Mao's revolutions, for example, began as idealistic movements against oppression, only to end up being myriad times more oppressive. On an individual level, abused children not infrequently grow into abusive parents; sexually molested kids may age into sexually maladjusted adults. If only one could help find a way to stop this intergenerational transmission of wounds — this bequeathing of human misery — that could be as valuable as his work at Amnesty. To try some such experiment along these lines was why he moved to a place like Crestone, where everything was not already set in stone.

As for how to (and who will) heal this transmission of wounds, James is creating Peace Ambassadors.* He teaches, via the internet, the necessary skills to become healing presences, and some travel to Crestone to be mentored by him in his home. A thousand such Peace Ambassadors in thirty countries are now working on healing their personal wounds while endeavoring to ameliorate the communal wounds around them; theirs is a nonduality of self and society, put to practical uses.

After working in Washington, James searched for some progressive place where spirituality or politics, awareness or action, are not *or*, where he could try melding them into a new synthesis that attempts what realpolitik by itself cannot achieve. His sister worries that he is too isolated in Crestone, but he is not alone. A not negligible percentage of the population here believes, or wants to believe, that something untried is yet possible: that not in differences hotly acted on but in subtle affinities affirmed lies the last best hope of the world.

James thus did not retreat to Crestone to escape from society's problems; rather he planned to use Crestone as a home

---

* What exactly is a Peace Ambassador? Robert Gurung is an example. When Bhutan expelled its immigrant workers, Robert's family got herded into semipermanent refugee camps in Nepal. Incensed, young Robert determined that he would one day retaliate against Bhutan by assassinating its king. But then he chanced on one of James's books, and his ambition changed. He would not live as a victim. Mentored personally by James, Robert is now writing a book tentatively called *From Revenge to Realization*. That could define a Peace Ambassador — one conducting diplomatic negotiations to arrange for retaliation a safe passage to reconciliation.

base from which he would waltz around the world, teaching personal growth conjoined with social healing through conscious activism. His first years here he did just that, when for him the other side of the coin of Crestone was here, there, and everywhere: from Micronesia to Turkey, from Ireland to Japan: name a place where he could teach the keys to personal and collective peace, and he would be there. Though soon enough he would come to be haunted by a reading in the *I Ching* called "Mountain Arresting Progress." Did the Sangre de Cristos arrest his? Previously, at Amnesty, working in the world's wounded places, he had encountered practically every bitter sorrow known to humankind. Now, though, he tasted the bitterness within himself.

When I first knew James no one noticed — it didn't interfere — but now it's too obvious to be a secret. He has Parkinson's disease. On those mornings when his body is like an alien object, unwieldy and with its own perverse will, he rails against whatever powers there be, "Why did you inflict this upon your servant?" Parkinson's is associated with depression (hardly surprising), and in bad moments sadness about his situation wells up, poisoning those moments.

James, not one to coddle himself, though, tries to shed every vestige of self-pity or despairing darkness within (not always successfully), to not let anything hinder his ability to benefit others and to grow personally. He recalls those Sufi masters in Turkey who broke through every personal reference point to realize an abundance of being beyond qualification. Recently James composed a Soul Awakening Prayer (and is writing a book to accompany it), which is meant to be recited three times — once for oneself *or* another, then for oneself *and* another, and finally for all the world, including oneself. Within the ordeals of Parkinson's, James has found on the far side of sorrow, in the mystic Ibn Arabi's words, "the garden among the flames."

The idea of nonduality has become, oddly, strangely fashionable in some spiritual circles. As Meg was when she first heard of it, James is put off by its easy I-am-you-ness and its simplistic one-essence-in-all. Yet what is a "garden among the flames," even symbolically, if not a form of nonduality; what is bitter = sweet, sweet = bitter, if not nonduality? The bitter: in different months during the coming year (that I am writing this) two of his three sons will get married, and James had to inform them that his misbehaving body could not RSVP that it would attend. The sweet: that being the case, each son replied, he and his bride would hold a second ceremony in Crestone, and that ceremony, with him present, would be the true blessing on their union. Ramloti (whom we will meet in chapter 12) will conduct the ceremony at the Haidakhandi Ashram, it will be a fire ceremony, as in India marriages have been consecrated for millennia.

The last time I was with James he said that, with death now thinkable, he had decided what he wants on his tombstone besides his name. Which is a single word. That word, *Integrity* (he qualifies it, *if true*) is to indicate that what he has known inside himself and what he has shown the world are one and the same. When I left, James said goodbye the way Sequoyah Trueblood does when leaving James's house: "We will always be connected."

NEAR-ENLIGHTENMENT EXPERIENCES IN EVERYDAY LIFE

11. The Look of It, the Feel of It

T he subject of enlightenment ushers us into the book's finale: for enlightenment (though sometimes designated by other words*) is reckoned the last station stop on the spiritual journey. When well along on that journey, the transformation — the realization, the butterfly emerging from the chrysalis — that Tsoknyi Rinpoche foretold (see chapter 3) becomes felt reality. You begin to realize such unexpected ease, depths of empathy, and unblinkered awareness that it may seem you have practically entered another way of being, one so extraordinary that Tsoknyi dubbed it, perhaps tongue in cheek, beyond human.

---

* What word, for instance? Here's a surprising synonym. When pressed for a synonym for *enlightenment*, James O'Dea responded: *selfless service*. The irony is that in selfless service the self is fulfilled. That irony makes sense, James believes, when we recognize that our original nature, or essence, is enlightened, before it gets all muddied over with ignominious adaptations and compromises. Our original or divine essence is what James's Sufi philosopher Ibn Arabi tried to evoke when he wrote, "Creation allowed God to have a mirror in which to behold his beautiful names [qualities]." The godhead's beautiful names are many of the same names — Compassion, Positive Vision, Free Will, Necessity, Imagination, Generosity, Sacredness, etc. — of the rungs on the ladder to enlightenment we'll climb in the next chapter.

But what's wrong with "simply" being a human healthy in body and outlook? Isn't it sufficient to grow ever more capable, thoughtful, loving, and generous (regardless of that doomed boat party at life's end)? There is nothing *wrong* with it; to the contrary, everyone should harbor such an ambition. Accomplishment, love, generosity represent the pinnacle achievements of a human life; they (and kindred felicities) give us reasons to be happy. But what happens if those reasons take a tumble or begin to crumble? To be happy with no reason at all seems counterintuitive — why? how? — is it even possible?

To compare the two kinds of happiness, with and without reasons, let's momentarily leave Crestone and meet two people once at the top of their game, renown and acclaim following them like a shadow. The world was their oyster, until...

The Pulitzer Prize–winning historian Tony Judt was considered "one of the best-known public intellectuals in America," the "liveliest mind in New York." Until... 2009, when he suffered total paralysis from the neck down. His happiness and his reasons for it miserably vanished under the merciless onslaught of ALS (Lou Gehrig's disease). Now compare Judt with the Vietnamese monk Thich Nhat Hanh under similarly dire circumstances. Thich Nhat Hanh — called "the voice of the Buddha in our time," nominated by Martin Luther King for the Nobel Prize — fared in some ways even worse. Unlike Judt, after his stroke Thich Nhat Hanh could no longer even speak: he could do little more than breathe. Could he meditate, I wondered, since that just involves consciously breathing in and out? Evidently he could — and did. Months later, when he finally managed to utter four meager syllables, he reported, "In...Out...Happy." Happy regardless of (even devastating) conditions: happy (as Tsoknyi says) without a reason.

Enlightenment may be, simply, happiness with no reason. It is also to journey as far as humanly/beyond-humanly possible in the direction of compassion. Simultaneously to go the complete distance in clarity, in unobstructed awareness. But how can ordinary people, you and I, effect this abracadabra? Enlightenment may happen in the midst of the everyday, but it is not an everyday occurrence: How, oh how, to flip on the light switch?

Enlightenment pundits are not much help, rarely descending from clouds of generalization to delineate it in actual detail — it's all left so vague, some inner Shangri-la of the psyche. In this chapter and especially the next, however, as some Crestonians strut their stuff on the stage of strangeness, we will investigate *what* it is, not in theory, not as an abstract ideal, but as it is lived out in daily, mundane details, even in a Colorado mountain town. When Tulku Thondup discussed enlightenment in his bestselling *The Healing Power of Mind*, he interjected, "But before this gets too complicated, let me say there are many people alive on the Earth now who are partly enlightened." Are any Crestonians *partly* enlightened? And would juxtaposing the enlightened parts of this one and of that dovetail, as in a jigsaw puzzle, into something like the whole picture?

Looking the Part

Were enlightenment a sexy subject for a movie, Crestone might provide some set locations. The town — or a few residents here — looks the part, the stereotypical image of the seeker (or of the oddball). I don't suppose the few examples below are enlightened, but they at least make Crestone look like a place where it could happen.

See that wispy figure with the gray beard down to his waist — surely a Taoist sage or Buddhist recluse? His cave-like hut perches less than a mile above the town ("as the crow flies"), but you need a guide to find it as you ford streams while keeping an eye out for bears and mountain lions. Yeshe Dorje — American man, Tibetan name — has meditated in solitude there for fifteen years, having prepped by previously meditating in solitude in Nepal for fifteen years. Yeshe has a cell phone, though, which connects to the internet and keeps him, when he's not meditating, so au courant that he could advise you on anything (except the stock market). I recently phoned Yeshe, hoping to visit again, but he apologized: not this week, this was a crazy-busy week. *Busy?* If you've been holed up alone for decades in a time beyond time — busy with what?

Occasionally rumors waft down from his hut: for example, a beautiful young woman climbed up there one day, and now they are engaged. Yeshe frequently travels to Nepal to look after his hundred-year-old teacher, Chatral Rinpoche, whom Thomas Merton called "the greatest man I ever met." Okay, say you have been meditating and taming your destructive emotions for half of forever: With what result? Some folks here consider Yeshe still a most difficult person.

If so, then thank god for the meditation, for what might he be like without it?

If hiking to inaccessible mountain huts is not your ticket to bliss, there's a village yogi you can see right in town. Raggedy, barefoot, ill-kempt, each year he looks a bit worse for wear. Nearing seventy, David Harding resembles a Hindu ex-householder who, having completed his family duties (he has eight grown children), has retired to the forest for contemplation. David's "forest" is a wreck of a trailer, in which he dreams of enlightenment in this lifetime. Along the way marijuana (in moderate amounts) and beer (in bottomless-pit amounts) are allowed. He was quietly drinking beer in Crestone's little city park a few months ago, when a police car from nearby Saguache, sirens sounding, came screeching to a stop beside him. Out poured an obese policeman, who clapped the drinking-in-public miscreant in handcuffs and began beating him, while calling on his two-way radio for reinforcements. During the beating and the painful handcuffed ride to Saguache, Dave kept laughing: *So this is my karma. Here's my chance to practice patience.* Before his trial Dave instructed his friends to wish the policeman no harm and to hold no grudge against him.

Of those here who look as though they emerged from some Himalayan cave, my favorite is Yochi. For the past fifteen years Yochi (pronounced *yo-see*) has inhabited not a cave but an abandoned mine shaft in the mountain's stony rockface. Mine shafts being damp, Yochi often sleeps outside in a hammock under blankets, even in subfreezing weather. He goes about barefoot until it's too cold, when he puts on socks, which freeze, and then he glides on them like skis. To my knowledge Yochi practices no particular religion, yet there's a shy retiring Bhutanese scholar in town who treks out to visit him to learn what a modern-day yogi is like.

I first spied Yochi one rare night on the porch of the Bliss. He was off sitting in a corner, which seemed to confirm that hermits are antisocial (in fact, he isn't). A bear was rummaging through the garbage cans out back, which furnished the pretext to start a conversation. "Say, Yochi, know any good bear stories?" He did, but unlike an ancient yogi, he got out a tiny tape recorder and created a file, "Bear Stories," into which to record his anecdotes. I especially liked the one about the bear who would come sleep near him. At one point Yochi told me that he also had spiritual stories. "Oh, really?" I replied. "I wouldn't mind hearing those." Not now, Yochi explained, he was in the "Bear Stories" file on his recording device.

After that night, when I'd see him on the road I'd give him a lift back to where his ascent to the mine shaft began. "Why do you live in a mine shaft?" I eventually asked. The rent was good. He had never excelled at making money, Yochi said, so finally he gave up trying. He would like to rent or use the other abandoned mine shafts near his — but for what purpose? Just to say something I suggested that, providing they were not too cold and damp, he might make them available to visiting spiritual practitioners as meditation caves. Or, alternatively, grow Cordyceps in them, a fungus with supposed aphrodisiac qualities that was reaping fortunes in the Himalayas. Yochi dug out from his bag a ballpoint pen and paper and began taking notes and thanked me for the privilege of talking with a sage.

Only gradually did I glean that Yochi lived in a mine shaft for reasons other than that the price was right. One day when pesky mosquitoes were feasting on us, Yochi wouldn't swat them because he "wanted to keep his karma clean." Another time when I gave him a ride, he was bearing a homemade sign that announced "In Silence." Apart from meditating and not killing animals, his dream is, it turns out, to fill the shafts, which are natural refrigerators, with beans and rice and other nonperishable foodstuffs. That way if ever a disaster hits, Crestone will have a food supply.

He seemed the sort of person you could say or ask anything to. Even: "Yochi, what is the greatest revelation you've had this year?" He praised me for posing such a wondrous question. He had to scrupulously calculate, though, what were the revelations of the past months and which belonged to earlier. At last he reported his insight. "To solve today's problems," Yochi said after long deliberation, "we should start a 'wave of love' that eventually will exclude nobody." It sounded like hippie wisdom from Haight-Ashbury, yet it is actually something he could do (and he probably does). As Galaxy described him, "Yochi wears a pure heart on his shirt-sleeve."

What Yochi and Yeshe Dorje and David Harding do is provide a background that makes enlightenment look like something that could happen here, and would you care to try? Most other places half resemble the kingdom in the parable, where the water supply is evilly poisoned, causing whoever drinks it to go insane. The king, forewarned, refrains, but to his insane subjects, he appears deranged, so he has no choice but to drink the lunatic water, too. Because of Crestone's wider or wilder spectrum of mind-sets, should enlightenment ever befall anyone here, it might not constitute grounds for being committed. The king would not have to swallow the waters of oblivion.

Aside. Enlightenment would seem to suit a small, overcrowded planet running out of supplies. An enlightened person's (e.g., the Buddha's, Jesus's) version of well-being — in contrast to the egotist's — involves needing less materially rather than more. In capitalism's foundational text, *The Wealth of Nations* (1776), Adam Smith proposed that, if everybody pursued his own personal gain, those pursuits would neatly dovetail into a functioning, prosperous society. Maybe then, maybe in privileged societies in Europe or America; less true today for an ever more depleted, interconnected planet, where a tiny minority hogs what the large majority needs. The road to enlightenment has its departure point supposedly when one thinks of others' needs on a par with, if not before, one's own. Along the way, the dream of single-generation, self-centered reality is awoken from.

The Feel of It

Is Tsoknyi Rinpoche enlightened? He would dismiss it as a silly question. Anyone even partly enlightened will, to avoid feeding the ego, deny it more fiercely than if they had been accused of a crime. In this regard an eminent Tibetan teacher (Anam Thubten), visiting here, announced his new mantra:

"I'm a bunch of baloney." But then anyone who is not enlightened, except a charlatan, would also deny it. So how can
we discern who might be?

Even if he is not enlightened, Tsoknyi does exhibit three
characteristics often associated with enlightened beings. First
of all, he no longer covets what most people deem the summum bonum — a personal, gratifying life on his own terms.
As detailed earlier, no longer does he crave any private time
to himself or strictly personal satisfactions. Many people par-
tition experience into either work and chores or relaxation,
either imposed obligations or doing what one wants. But
Tsoknyi does not side with one or the other. Such not-siding
and not-craving may be a job requirement for doing what he
does. Spiritual teachers, like good mothers, are supposed to
think of the welfare of those in their care before they do of
their own.*

Second, he is happy without needing a reason to be. His
days may plunge him into the vicarious purgatories of others'
problems and despair, but his equitable good nature does not
go into hiding, even as he enters their worlds of woe. And
probably others' suffering, and his composure while he attempts to ameliorate it, need to coexist, lest he drown in a sea
of ineffectual commiseration.

As I am writing this, Tsoknyi Rinpoche has just returned

---

*   Yet if he could do absolutely anything he desired — with his desire being the sole
     consideration — he would be meditating in a cave. Instead, he recently completed
     a five-year, seven-million-dollar project (what a lot of onerous fund-raising that
     involved) of building in his childhood town of Nubri a school for girls from Nepal
     and India who otherwise would be living on the streets. That is one of his projects
     among many.

from Nepal, where he may have set the Guinness record for worst case of diarrhea. For weeks it raged until he could barely stand; on top of that he had a nasty, virulent flu. His physical condition inconvenienced him but his mood, or possibly his "subtle body," was fine and full of ease. Tsoknyi may experience more well-being when sick than most people do when well.

Enlightenment's third characteristic involves the most misused word in the English language. What Tsoknyi means by *freedom*, however, is not what smarmy politicians mean. Freedom for him refers to not clinging, to not being enslaved by one's inner compulsions. For then what genuine liberty would you have?

Tsoknyi still clings. He clings to the beneficial, clings to success for the charitable projects he undertakes. He hopes one day, though, not to grasp on to even the good. He wants eventually not to be compassionate (personally empathizing with another's misfortune) so much as to *become* compassion, that is, for it to spontaneously infuse his every thought and gesture. During the Q and As in his last retreat an old woman asked Tsoknyi what he meant when he said such-and-such, when in fact he had never said anything remotely like it. People got angry at her for not paying attention and wasting everyone's time. (It turned out that she was largely deaf.) Tsoknyi studied her for a moment, and though he hadn't said what she thought he did, he replied, "A very good question. Here's what I meant when I said such-and-such." He did not cling to his point, crucial though it was, but sacrificed it to make another fallible person feel good in herself.

As for whom to emulate on the road to enlightenment,

Tsoknyi may be too good a model to serve as a model. After all, he trained from early childhood on in how to emigrate to the land beyond self-referential, personal concerns. Let us study the great ones, certainly, but let us not neglect the more modest examples we might actually hope to replicate.

About the few people in Crestone who might conceivably fit Tulku Thondup's description of being partly enlightened: if we took each one's quite different fragment of embodied compassionate understanding, could we, step by step, construct a kind of ladder ascending to a glimpse of the whole? The last chapter of this book will attempt to climb that imagined ladder and to survey — to the extent that it is on view in Crestone — the panorama of human realization and fulfillment.

12. Nine Rungs Up the Ladder to Enlightenment

Want to sail beyond the ocean of suffering? If enlightenment — that inner transformation that supposedly replaces misery with well-being — is your goal, would a sojourn in Crestone expedite it (or not)?

To respond to that impossible-to-answer-directly question, let's bump into some likely townsfolk whom we often run across (some of whom we've met before), except now we'll regard them in a different light and with a more probing eye. We'll slyly scan for what in them fosters happiness, compassion, and awareness while defusing the opposites. I have identified nine enlightenment attributes among the men and women here: hence nine remarkable stories, nine rungs up our ladder to enlightenment. *Nine?* — that's too many to keep straight, so let's cluster them around a few genres of enlightenment experience.

Malleability

By a certain age one's career (or lack thereof), intimate relationships (or lack thereof), and one's thought patterns can appear fixed in place, objective "givens." As one edges closer to an enlightened viewpoint, though, a great unloosening begins, making the day's contours and contents adaptable to reshaping to a different meaning or use. Thus your world internally (but not only internally) becomes more flexible, more workable. Even opposites, antonyms — reality versus imagination or free will versus necessity — from that larger perspective may become allied, if not exactly synonymous. (The first two rungs of our ladder provide the illustration.)

Rung One: Reality in the Mirror of Imagination

EXEMPLAR: GALAXY

Certainly her parents did not burden Galaxy with that moniker, and anybody rebaptizing herself Galaxy must be one New Age flake. Except this Galaxy (whom we earlier met camping in the mountains) is sensible, feet squarely on the ground, a former university professor. At a retreat she attended everyone was instructed to take a new name, unassociated with the habits and limitations of their old identity. *Galaxy*, hardly a person's name, came unbidden to her mind, and she was reluctant to adopt it, even temporarily. I need a sign, she thought, not knowing what would constitute one. That summer's evening, seventeen shooting stars streaked through the sky. Good enough; Galaxy she was.

Eventually the 24/7 demands of college teaching in academia, more and more being run like a business, led Galaxy to conclude: *enough*. To be truthful, depression also played a part in her leaving the university. She was ready to consider anything that helped to lift that leaden weight — what did she have to lose? A far cry from academic respectability, coming to Crestone she demoted, or promoted, herself to being a cook at one of the spiritual centers (Vajra Vidya).

Her breakthrough from depression came, unexpectedly, when unaccountably she began having visions of Kali. When Galaxy was feeling oppressed, an image of Kali — the Hindu goddess of terrifying demeanor, breathing flame and fire — would come to mind, and strangely, the problem would lessen. Once, for example, in a communal camping area a man was stalking her, perhaps sensing in a depressed woman an easy victim. Galaxy then pictured Kali sweeping the vicinity clean, and shortly thereafter the creep ceased bothering her. Imagining a terrifying goddess may have caused her own demeanor to change, which in turn caused the stalker to back off.

But she was no Hindu, so why was she spontaneously conjuring Kali and, odder yet, why was doing so of some benefit? No matter: After that incident at the campsite she replaced the *Is it true?* with *Does it help?* The difference between reality and a hallucination, the poet Shelley said, was how long it lasted. The difference between a fantasy and a vision, Galaxy decided, was how much good it worked.

It was when her depression began to abate that Galaxy met John Milton and relocated to Crestone, coveting a more sacramental relation to her surroundings. How do you achieve a sense of sanctity, if it wasn't early on ingrained in Sunday school? Now, say, if Galaxy spied a dead coyote in the road, she would slam on the brakes, get out of the car, and carry the carcass into a field. What difference did it make, since the coyote was dead? But allowing cars all day to run over a creature formerly free and having carried the breath of life would not show proper respect, she felt, for it as a part of a creation possibly divine. Another example: In a nature retreat that Galaxy leads for teenagers, her assignment to them was to create sacred space. One boy terrified of bears put up six-foot poles over a mound of bear poop as a shrine, which had the effect of lessening his fear of them. Such simple actions, done with sanctity in mind, changed those kids' attunement to their environment.

During Galaxy's twenty-eight-day retreat above Crestone (see chapter 7), imagination and reality became strangely complementary fields of experience. She had no business up there to distract her as she felt the nature around her wordlessly enfolding her, causing a subtle shift in her sense of identity — as when one goes from, say, living alone to attending a family reunion. After the twenty-eight days as a (real or imagined) integral part of nature, she felt herself an altered person. As such, she descended into a Crestone that, with her changed vision, beckoned like the city at the end of the quest. Such an avalanche of structures, inventions, enterprises, commodities, activities, people, cars, and rush. Amazing to her was the collective imagination it had taken to assemble, out of a once unpopulated landscape, such a wonder town. *Can something become sacred,* she wondered, *simply by our hearts thinking it is?*

Rung Two: The Confluence of Free Will and Necessity

EXEMPLAR: "D."*

Many a year D. has lived in Crestone, but her breakthrough insight occurred elsewhere, while she was vacationing in India. That country, which one supposedly either loves or

---

* D. is obviously an initial and in this case not even the correct initial. She requested that her actual name not be used. Anonymity in little Crestone? — that may require more than a name/initial change.

hates, left her indifferent; nor was she bashful in voicing her distaste. In Rajkot she challenged the travel agent, "Besides Gandhi's old ashram, does this crummy town boast anything worth a second or even a first glance?" "Most affirmative!" replied the travel agent. "The Ramakrishna Monastery. Everything else in Rajkot is the shit of the bull."

When D. phoned the monastery, a monk invited her for tea, surely a pro forma courtesy. When she at last ambled over, however, the monk had been waiting for her with tea for six hours. "Esteemed Guest, does our poor country please you?" came the inevitable question. "What do you think of Holy Mother India?"

D., young and brash, thought India a nuthouse, with loonies worshipping idols, even giving them — just what a god wants [sarcasm] — milk baths. The sympathetic monk explained that attending to the deity's statue, the statue itself, was not necessary. Divinity is, however, so beyond human comprehension, the monk went on, that it is a kindness to provide something to settle the eyes on and to give your hands occupation. Gandhi, when his countrymen gushed, "Thank you for all you're doing for India!" would reply, "No, I'm doing it for myself." Likewise for religious observance, the monk said, we are doing it for ourselves.

Well, that made a little sense. India's hocus-pocus hodgepodge of alien rites was then not a worshipping of idols (gods) but a way of activating certain latent energies in the worshipper otherwise left dormant. A great shift in the inner life occurs — it was occurring for D. — when one progresses from venerating the outward forms to realizing the buddha or gnostic Christ within. Ultimately all outward forms of worship, the monk told D., may be arbitrary, but they can still improve our outlook and inspire us to better actions — "proof of the pudding!" the monk exclaimed — and in the process become necessary for us.

Once back in Crestone, D. had a different outlook about religious rituals and practices: even if they had originated as imaginative human creations, they could be validated or experienced — and thus become felt reality — through participating in their ceremonies and celebrations. Now when Buddhist rinpoches visited Crestone, though she considered herself Christian, D. no longer hesitated to prostrate before them. Prostration is only a gesture, after all. Such arbitrary gestures, she now saw, give elusive meaning form, and the form becomes presence, and presence makes the ineffable almost tangible.

Safety

As the ego feels less need to protect itself, ironically you may feel more protected. For then the hazards of happenstance do not land so hard: your refusal to take them personally frees you from feeling singled out, bereft and vulnerable. And should bad go to yet worse, the next two rungs of the ladder — devotion and compassion (or "putting another before you") — may inwardly safeguard you from worse's worst reverberations.

Rung Three: Devotion

EXEMPLAR: RAMLOTI

In the so-called spiritual life, how far could someone progress if she dispensed with the typical contents of the spiritual life? What kind of religious interiority would she have if she:

- had no belief in God (certainly not a paternalistic Jehovah or Allah)
- had no goal of enlightenment or the kingdom of heaven
- didn't necessarily do practices like meditation to get beyond the ego
- did not pour over religious texts?

Many would think, *Hope the poor sap is already happy, for she's not going anywhere.* Yet this person — if referring to a certain woman in Crestone — leads a completely fulfilling spiritual life. Her name is Ramloti (born Deborah Wood Guth, in 1949). And instead of immersing herself in the religious stocks-in-trade mentioned above, Ramloti concentrates on one: devotion.

"Devotion is not to a god or teacher," Dzongsar Khyentse, the Tibetan guru and filmmaker, said. "Devotion is to the formula *Cause + condition = results.*" *Cause* here is contact with transformative teachings, and *condition* is an undamaged mind receptive to considering them. And if the *result* is a small increment in feeling better in oneself, and if that happens repeatedly, then trust builds up and graduates into devotion.

Ramloti's cause was receiving unconditional love. The result, the form her devotion now takes, is to be as loving as possible herself. She is the director of the Haidakhandi Universal Ashram here, and anything visitors there want, she attempts to give to them. If they want food she gives food; if they want quiet to worship she leaves them alone; if they need to discuss their problems she is attentive. She remembers what it was like when she first experienced unconditional love.

That life-changing event took place more than three decades ago and plunged Debbie Guth into an experience, she felt, practically out of mythology. In 1970, in the Indian village of Haidakhan, there had appeared a beautiful young man who announced he was (the reincarnation of) Babaji. In Swami Yogananda's bestselling *Autobiography of a Yogi* (1946), the previous Babaji was the author's guru's guru's guru's guru's guru (give or take a guru), a figure or supposedly godhead lost in legend. Carl Jung dismissed *The Autobiography of a Yogi* as whipped-cream fluff; Steve Jobs, on the other hand, reread it every year. Few have responded to it as Debbie did, though, who, when she learned that Yogananda's Babaji had again manifested in time, cashed in her savings and booked a flight to India. When they met (the year was 1981), practically Babaji's first words to her were, "You not Debbie. You Devi. No, Ramloti." When Deborah-Devi-now-Ramloti learned that the latter meant "one who carries God inside always," she thought, *Since seeing you I do.*

Babaji did not view her, she felt, in a particular race (Caucasian), role (mother of three), nationality (American), profession (sales), or age or personality type. His X-ray gaze penetrated to her essence, to herself just as she was, without her biographical and cultural baggage. How freeing it was to be seen and accepted that way. Ramloti claims that Babaji never failed to know what she was thinking; there was thus no place to hide, but, she discovered, there was also no need to. One day he was planning to visit, and her desk was a mess, a hurricane wreckage of sloppiness, so — simple solution — she dumped the chaos into a file cabinet drawer. Babaji entered her room, marched straight to the file cabinet, opened precisely that drawer, and said, "I don't like."

What Ramloti didn't like was the fact that he gave five

other women disciples saris but not her. How unworthy she must be. She tumbled through the loops and hoops of self-condemnation until she realized, *My god, it's just a piece of cloth*, and besides, she didn't need another sari. The next day Babaji strode up to her and presented her with a golden one. When she wore that gold sari, perhaps distracted by pride, she tripped on it, spilling the tray of treats that Babaji liked to distribute. She dreaded looking up, as she heard Babaji say, "You hopeless lady." But when she did finally glance up, such loving tenderness was in his eyes, which nothing she did would likely diminish or increase. Unconditional love like his, she thought, is like a greenhouse for humans — the warmth and light in which we can grow.

Before Babaji died (in 1984) he exhorted disciples like Ramloti to found ashrams, centers of harmony, wherever possible. Serendipitously, an ocean and a continent away, Hanne Strong was offering free land to traditional religious groups and was only too pleased to add Hinduism to the spiritual smorgasbord. This was how a picturesque slice of Hindu India got transposed to a remote town in Colorado.

The ashram does not call itself Hindu, however, but rather the Haidakhandi *Universal* Ashram, for Babaji believed that, to survive, a world of conflicting beliefs must yield to cross-religious harmony. In its universal phase, the ashram plays well with others: when the Buddhists built their big stupa here, for example, the ashram cooked meals for those laboring Buddhists. In its Hindu aspect, Americanized Indians bring their families visiting from India to the ashram, where the parents practically sigh with relief: *Our children are not lost in a heathen land after all.* For Ramloti whether it is

Hindu or universal is beside the point. The point being love, devotion.

Should you care to witness this unadulterated devotion, free from all the quibbling, qualified *maybe*s of the modern mind, hike up to attend one of the many celebrations at the ashram. Go, say, for Navaratri, their nine-day celebration of the divine feminine. As the cool mountain mist mixes with eye-stinging smoke from the ritual fire, cloaked in haze and fog you step out of contemporary time into rituals going back thousands of years. Inside the main building the god Shiva has lost his head, in storybook legends being read to twenty-first-century children, tales that date back before the Bible, back before Greek mythology.

An intellectual might dismiss such rituals the way V. S. Naipaul did similar ancestral ceremonies in Hindu Trinidad: *Boring and interminable and the food came only at the end.* The cold-eyed Naipaul could not understand devotion because it was not intellectual. Devotion uncomplicates the modern mind, which ordinarily cannot stop projecting and worrying. At the Navaratri festival you may not comprehend the unfamiliar Hindu rituals or the Sanskrit mantras being chanted, but wrapped in mists and smoke, surrounded by families and by children playing, you can imbibe the life-as-piety all around you, and your heart may realize a peace that the mind never knows.

For those with temperaments amenable to it, devotion can provide an opening into, perhaps not enlightenment, but a satisfying alternative. It may lack the all-encompassing vision, but for much of the peace, joy, and empathy that enlightenment reportedly brings, devotion will do nicely.

Rung Four: *Putting Another Before You*

EXEMPLAR: MARK ELLIOTT

A great divide in humankind separates those who think of themselves first and those who think of others first. Recently I was the beneficiary of just such a person who puts others first, when I had, and didn't have, a heart attack.

The Heart Attack sutra. One evening a week ago I felt a pressure in my chest, a pulling sensation that were it anywhere else — an elbow would be good — you'd hardly notice it. But in the chest...that couldn't be, could it? ...I phoned the one doctor practicing (part-time) in Crestone, but since it was night she said to come to the office tomorrow. Do heart attacks wait? The internet was no more helpful because under symptoms of heart attack it lists, besides all the scary stuff I didn't have, an additional category: any other sensation in the chest area. There I was, alone with my fear, wondering whom I could call. Mark Elliott might know the symptoms, but he was doing a retreat with Tsoknyi, so I shouldn't bother him. Oh, what the hell; with apologies: I called. Without hesitation Mark responded, "Forget my retreat, this is nothing you take chances with." He insisted on driving me right away to the emergency room in Salida, though it was late and Salida was more than an hour away. Now here's a coincidence. Just that day during the retreat teachings Tsoknyi had said that to do *tonglen* (imaginatively taking on another's suffering) instead of actually driving them to the hospital in the next town — a worse betrayal of the dharma there could hardly be.

At the emergency room I was the sole customer, until three police cars hauled in a scraggily dwarf in ratty robes, to arrange a physical before incarceration. Most people would have recoiled from the man's filth and odor while wondering what crime he had committed. Mark's response, though, was to enter with sadness and sympathy into the poor man's situation. Soon enough I got a clean bill of health, but the doctor suggested I spend the night so they could do further stress tests in the morning. Uh-uh. I wanted out of even the friendliest hospital in America. Mark, though, was willing to forget the retreat and check into a motel and loan me his iPad if I wanted to stay. *The most sublime act* — that line of poetry came to my mind — *is to set another before you.*

The next day, this thought flashed through Mark's mind: *Damn. I left the retreat, drove all that way, and Jeff wasn't even having a heart attack.* He was immediately appalled at having entertained such an uncharitable thought, but later, when hearing it, I recalled Virginia Woolf's observation that at crises the wrong phrase invariably springs to mind. At the retreat the next day Mark castigated his shameful lack of generous feeling: "Maybe I have 3 percent compassion." Afterward, Tsoknyi joked to Esteban, "Mark was wrong — he probably has 6 percent." It was a joke, but if Mark has 6 percent, what would someone with 20 percent compassion do?

Congeniality

An ancient parable describes how the Buddha, in a previous lifetime, had one shoulder caressed by a beautiful woman and the other gnawed by a tiger and supposedly could not tell the difference. The parable's shortcoming is that, even as parables go, it's not believable: maybe a buddha is, but we *Homo sapiens* seem incapable of such a supermundane response. On the next rung of the ladder, however — One Taste — we observe on a far more modest scale someone for whom success and failure (lady and tiger) are experienced as not entirely dissimilar. Then on the rung after that we encounter two women who have domesticated the tiger nearly into a purring, declawed pet.

Rung Five: One Taste

EXEMPLAR: RALPH ABRAMS

One taste is the term for when unalike experiences register the same pleasant mild flavor. Such evenness of response to life's rough-and-tumble would help equalize or neutralize — and buffer you from — its overwhelming ups and downs, from its exhausting good-then-bad-then-good-then-bad (ad nauseam). But does true one taste actually occur, or is it just a pretty idea in spiritual books? Remember when I asked Tsoknyi Rinpoche if he ever felt pleasure and pain similarly and he responded, "I am not there yet, but I have tasted it." So maybe.

Here's another example. Ralph Abrams has done retreats and spiritual practice out the wazoo, but in 2011 he launched a telecom company. What if such dissimilar activities were for him not entirely dissimilar? Since he had zero experience with commercial computer technology, and had failed at businesses before, I doubted he could make a go of Crestone Telecom. By 2012, though, it had gone from being in the red to being in the black. Did his earlier spiritual practice leak, one taste–like, into his business approach? "Ralph," I said, "I'm writing this book on contemporary spirituality. Is there any way to make Crestone Telecom into the new Jesus?"

His reply? "Perhaps it is." Ralph was being his usual amusing self, but then he does not approach Crestone Telecom with the no-holds-barred ferocity of a thirty-year-old start-up entrepreneur. Indeed, it began as a nonprofit business. He realized that Crestone needed affordable high-speed access so that people here, where jobs are scarce, could work long-distance. Only when his grant proposal for funding internet in rural areas was rejected did Ralph convert Crestone Telecom into a for-profit business model. And only then did folks here take it seriously.

In his midsixties Ralph was now working long hours, but he made his day longer by rising at dawn to meditate. A notepad rested by his cushion in which to jot down his meditation-inspired insights for the business — so unlike the anxious thoughts that had jolted him out of bed an hour earlier. He was a businessman upset by setbacks and nervous about bank loans, but he was also a spiritual practitioner for whom ambition and detachment, and work and pleasure, did not exist in entirely unrelated spheres.

After years of meditation highs, Ralph felt he needed to counterbalance or at least solidify them. And so he plunged wholeheartedly into samsara, into the in-your-face everyday, first by running for mayor and then by starting the telecom business. Yet he plunged with a difference, as traces of his thirty-five years of spiritual practice seeped into Crestone Telecom. Ralph can be detached (sometimes) and view Crestone Telecom in quite disparate ways: as a calculated gamble to earn badly needed moola, as a contribution to the town's welfare, or even, in a flight of fantasy, as telecommunicative or interconnecting lines in the human mandala. None of those suggest "one taste," but in his good-humored flexibility to imagine them all, a faint flavor of it slips through. Ralph becomes downcast when a deal falls through and animated if one succeeds, but a day (or four or five) later, when he accepts either — for in each there's life and energy — a subtle hint of one taste steals in.

Recently nearby towns like Buena Vista and Salida have asked Ralph if he can replicate Crestone Telecom for them. After he made his presentation in Salida, a woman there surprised Ralph by observing, "Did you notice the love in the room?" It reminded him that the business had originated with a compassionate purpose as its goal. By importing love or goodwill into a hard-nosed meeting, Ralph had smuggled a taste of one taste right into the middle of a business conference.

Rung Six: Positive Vision

EXEMPLARS: BERTHA GOTTERUP; KATE "HAMIDA NUR" STEICHEN

We have heard Bertha answer the question, "How can you view everything so positively?" with "That's all there is." Can she really mean that? I could run the alphabet from *a* (apartheid, antisemitism) to *z* (zamindars, Zimbabwe's Robert Mugabe), stumbling at every letter on positive's opposite. The good may represent a minor fraction of the news reported, but on her channel it's the majority of what's being observed. More than that: Bertha can embrace even life's shortcomings and seeming failures through a lens that uncovers in most hardships a redemptive underside. And thus an old woman in the mountains accepts life's harsher occurrences, accepts the dark clouds, because they transpire on a wider spectrum of possible experience in an overlooked, vaster scheme of things.

Bertha is not the only compass needle in Crestone pointing, as it were, true north. Kate Steichen, for instance, was trained from childhood on, when seemingly bad things happened, to find an extenuating interpretation. (And as a Sufi, she adds a Muslim spice to the religious potpourri of Crestone.)

Her schooling in positive outlook commenced early, when her father got bounced from corporate regional office to regional office. The family could never long call any place home, but the children were not allowed to sigh and reminisce about the wonderful place left behind. Instead, they should talk about what was better about the place newly moved to. Years later, after she relocated to Crestone, Kate met a crazy wisdom teacher in nearby Saguache who furthered the positive mind-set training her mother had begun. Kate sought him out to learn about the internet, then in its infancy, but his main teaching, it turned out, was not the internet but positive vision. When she was around him Kate hesitated to complain about anything because he'd encourage her to embrace it. Once she slipped, though, and mentioned her terminally ill father, with whom she'd never gotten along and whom hadn't seen in years. The teacher instructed Kate, "Go tell your father you love him," which gave her practically an allergic reaction. When she did begrudgingly visit, however, her father was elated. In a weak voice her dying father whispered, "Today, September 12, is a great day to be born."

Sufism would further her progress in positive vision. She learned about that mystical branch of Islam when Shaykha Fariha, the head of an international Sufi order, visited Crestone. Fariha asked those sitting around the small room, "What do you want — want more than anything else in the world?"

What Kate wanted was to shrink behind a chair or hide under the rug. For the answer that popped into her mind was — how embarrassing — *I want to be the deliriously happy slave of Allah.* She worried that such a desire could cost her everything.

What was she imagining — that if her response leaked out she would forfeit other people's respect? Kate had been a high achiever from the word go: two years out of college she ran the largest art school in New England; then she earned her MBA from Harvard; next she worked as a consultant to Fortune 500 companies. And now her next career move would be — slave of Allah? What could be more pathetic?

But on second thought — Kate immediately leaped to the second thought — what could be better? "Surrender" is one meaning of the word *islam*. In Shakya Fariha's Sufism one surrendered worries, obsessions, and, the greatest surrender of all, one's limited view. Islamic surrender resembles the Buddhist ideal of liberation, except that it's easier to achieve. Spiritual goals are always easier if a god (Allah) is in the vicinity to give you a leg up. Since she was surrendering to Allah, she added on a name that Allah would be more familiar with: Kate *Hamida Nur* Steichen.

Although Sufism can be American New Agey, Shaykha Fariha taught the Koranic bedrock — *sharia, tariqa, Al-Haqq, ma'rifa* — and she promised something more wondrous than

Rumi's intoxicated ecstasy. Better than dancing deliriously under the starry heavens, Fariha said, is simply to follow a path of gratitude. Gratitude can turn the misfortune knocking at your door into a welcome visitor. When uninvited guests — former friends who had cheated her out of money — showed up at a party Kate was giving, she (under Fariha's influence) determined not to get angry but to be grateful for their presence and use the opportunity to forgive them. And, as quickly as that, her resentment was over, and the party more fun than she thought possible. Surrender had promised a positive view *in spite of* whatever happened, and now gratitude made for a rosy outlook almost *because of* it.

Yet for all her gratitude, were one to ask Kate, "How can you view everything as positive?" her answer, unlike Bertha's, would be, "I don't." But she would add, "Not yet, anyway." Positive vision, she believes, may validate itself, for, instead of a negative so-called realism claiming to be the last bitter word on the subject, it usually leaves you healthier and happier.

Sacredness

Holiness, considering anything holy, almost no matter what it is, tends to lend it acceptability. Martyrs have demonstrated that even dying, if for a cause considered holy, need not be something to dread. If considering it sacrosanct can do that for death, then imagine how it might enhance our ideas of love and happiness and service. At a certain point of the spiritual path, so it's said, the path itself becomes the teacher. Everything encountered, all that transpires, favorable or unfavorable, becomes grist for practice. The following three people — the last three rungs — may be approaching that point where nearly everything appears sacred, qualified failures turn into qualified successes, and, worry not, for now there's no turning back.

Rung Seven: Hallowed Ground

EXEMPLAR: OSSIAN

Occasionally I'd drive out to the old silver Airstream trailer parked by Hanne's house. Inhabiting its small cave-like interior was Ossian, who spends twenty-four hours a day there, sleeping, eating, and mainly meditating. Ossian boasts a rather unusual claim to fame. According to *Newsweek* magazine, he was the first Westerner (he was born in 1967) to be recognized as a Buddhist rinpoche or high-ranking reincarnation. In this lifetime, his parents were hippie nobility who when Ossian was a small boy moved, it's said at his insistence, to Kathmandu. There the great 16th Karmapa broke precedent by recognizing as a Buddhist reincarnated rinpoche a Western boy. Some claim the Karmapa's recognition was an act of kindness, meant to extricate the child from his wild parents. (His father had been a drummer in the Velvet Underground, the band started by Andy Warhol, and which his father quit for being too conventional.)

Reincarnation is mainly an Eastern concept; *rinpoches* occur only within the Tibetan Buddhist tradition. *American rinpoche* is thus an oxymoron. Such a paradoxical figure provoked my curiosity, and finally I indulged it by asking the indirect question, "Ossian, what has been the key event in your life?"

"The crucial event for me," Ossian answered matter-of-factly, "was being born." Huh? I mean, sure, that's a big one, but...But if you believe the rinpoche business, then to reincarnate or imprint your consciousness into a new human form, and to do this to benefit your fellow creatures, would be the high point of your life, though occurring just prior to its beginnings. Arriving here "not in entire forgetfulness... but trailing clouds of glory" (Wordsworth), a rinpoche makes that prenatal decision, and everything subsequently falls in place semiautomatically.

When he was a baby, Ossian said, he would stare into his mother's eyes, trying to let her know who he was. By the time he was three he was babbling about Asia, to implant the notion in his parents to relocate there. When they did move to Kathmandu, little Ossian would beg his parents, "Take me to my monastery." As far-fetched as all this sounds, Ossian obviously believes it and in the whole rinpoche possibility. What's even odder, he makes you think that maybe, just maybe, his is what a reincarnated intelligence would be like, if such was possible.

How does a (supposed) rinpoche pass his days in, of all places, an old Airstream trailer? Ossian's first act at dawn is to meditate on Tara, the divine feminine, in case in negligent dream-sleep he overlooked saying his prayers to her. His prayers and meditations continue throughout the day as he simultaneously takes small sips of beer or inhales hits of marijuana mixed with tobacco. Is that a way for him to bring boundless sky-like consciousness down to Earth? Or maybe he simply enjoys it. Admiring women one after another fall in love with Ossian and hike out to the Airstream to reform him, and eventually leave, they unsuccessful and he unreformed. Occasionally Ossian wanders into town, where he may pick up at the Free Box a kitschy picture of Jesus and then hang it on the trailer's wall, like an icon.

For those who believe he is a rinpoche, he is one version of what a twenty-first-century holy man is like. For those who think, *rinpoche sminpoche*, he is the dope-smoking child of hippies. Ossian might rebut both hypotheses: *You went to all the magical bother of being born — and you're* still *making these sacred-profane distinctions?* Those are distinctions that an ordinary person, someone for whom some things are holy and others are not, would make. Ossian's mind seems at home, whether the subject is sacred or mundane. One moment he is discussing esoteric truths, the next pop trivia, as though both were equally commonplace and both equally holy. For Ossian, I gathered, anywhere, any situation, may be hallowed ground if you see it as such, and actions you do there are compassionate, especially when thoughts spontaneously arising there are helpful.

My assessment in this matter is qualified, however, for evidently Ossian smokes some *good shit*. That day, when I finally left it was dark, and in my altered state for the life of me I could not find my car, though it was parked but yards away. I fumbled back to the trailer to have Ossian guide me to it. That was the night I was most grateful for the quiet and emptiness of Crestone, not another automobile on the road for me to run into.

Rung Eight: Nonself, or Inner Spaciousness

EXEMPLAR: NORA TUNNEY SCHREIBER

Growing up, Nora Tunney's (b. 1955) experience of religion was a happy one, church was a pleasure, God a comfort. The beauty, the rituals, and the mystery of the Catholic religion all gratified the young Irish girl. The oldest of twelve children in a tiny house, she craved privacy, a sphere apart, and the church — both the building and the theology — supplied her refuge. At Catholic school she noticed nuns wearing wedding rings, and wondered, *How is that possible?* One nun explained to her, "I will tell you a great secret. I am married to God." Nora determined then and there to become a nun: after all, she could hardly hope for a better match.

Like Zoe and Ralph she also had a spontaneous awakening, when one moment to the next left her changed to the very core. Except her awakening happened in two separate parts. She remembers the date of the first: July 22, 1985. The topsy-turvy enthusiasms of the sixties had arrived in Ireland quite late and bounced Nora from nursing school to acting school to organic gardening in the Orkney Islands, a whirligig at times fueled by recreational drugs. But the hippie way to wisdom, instead of leading to a new fulfillment, caused Nora to feel empty and desperate for — *something*.

On that warm July day she was loitering on a bridge near a Trappist monastery in rural Ireland, daydreaming about this and that. The one undeniable fact of life, it suddenly struck her, was how intimately interconnected everything was. There she was standing alone on a footbridge but at the same time in a universe where every part, the sky, the trees, and herself, too, fit together like members of a large family. How simple. How wonderful. She was crying and laughing simultaneously, and her body felt as though it might combust with sheer happiness. A monk came strolling down the path, and not wanting to spoil her euphoria with talk, she hid behind a tree. She spied on the monk as he bent down and told a snail how beautiful it was. He greeted trees and flattered them shamelessly by telling them how bonny they were.

Nora stepped out from behind her tree and greeted the monk. The monk proceeded to tell her about the snailishness of God, about the treeishness of God, and, after he learned her name, about the Noraness of God. On the spot she beseeched the monk to become her teacher. Father Albrecht agreed, but on one condition: Nora must spend much of each day in meditation, in stillness, welcoming whatever was, wherever she was.

It turned out that Nora had a talent for solitude. She was never lonely, instead feeling kinship with all that was near and far away, too. Word about her spread, and the Carmelites, who established Nada Hermitage here, asked Nora to go live and pray for all humankind in a vacant monastery they had purchased in Ireland. In 1998 the Carmelites transferred Nora to their hermitage in Crestone, which is how she got there.

Once here she had the sense, as Bertha had earlier, that she'd finally arrived home. (Later, when the Carmelites wanted to post her elsewhere, she flatly refused.) She enjoyed monastery life at Nada, yet in many ways she had gone beyond it. Once she had needed monastic solitude to be inwardly still, once she had required it for the silence, but now she could experience stillness and quiet in the midst of activity. When she put on her nun's habit, she felt she was dressing up in theatrical costume, acting a role. Though it pained her to leave so sweet a hermitage, long before she left it physically she had already left it.

To be truthful, another reason also compelled her to renounce her vows. It concerned a man, Russell Schreiber, who was even more of a recluse than she. What happens when two hermits wed? Ordinarily, people marry for sexual gratification or to have children or for financial arrangements or because they cannot manage on their own or it's the socially acceptable thing to do. In their case the bond between them seemed a fait accompli — in the subtle interconnection among all things, they were especially connected — so it would have felt odder not to marry. Yet they were opposites in so many ways — he was meticulous and detailed and she, the contrary — but each's semiconscious idiosyncrasies flushed the other's into the open, and, made visible, those quirks often dropped away.

In 2009 the second half of her spontaneous awakening occurred. Nora had gone with a Finnish woman friend to the Haidakhandi Ashram to chant, though ordinarily she didn't like chanting. At the ashram without any forewarning she suffered a stroke, the life force ebbing out of her. In a garbled, nearly incomprehensible voice she whispered to her friend that she was dying but it was perfectly all right. Then everything went black.

It certainly had all the symptoms of a stroke, but, strangely, the next day Nora awoke recovered and was fine. Yet her center, her sense of a self, was gone; she was still Nora but without anything within her that could be pinpointed or felt as Noraness. When she went walking with Russell, her brain was not mapping her movements, it seemed; walking simply happened. Her mind wasn't deciding what to say so much as talking was happening. There was so much freedom in this way of being, for nothing needed to be taken personally. The seeker in her who had strained for years, winding herself tight, sleeping little, and feeling worn out from the constant quest, all that simply fell away.

What follows when a sense of space replaces a sense of the self? Nora's past year was, by any objective measure, an annus horribilis. Her beloved husband, Russell, died not long after being diagnosed with metastasized cancer, and Nora herself had to have a lung surgically removed. When Russell received the diagnosis, she was in Ireland, where he emailed her, "We will have to be very clever about this." He was never upset and, though his form of cancer typically causes great pain, oddly, he rarely felt any.

Russell's death would be expected to have unloosed in Nora a flood of tears and grief — but what if there is no ego to do the grieving? Nora's mourning both fit and did not fit the stereotype. If she recalled a memory of Russell, sorrow would well up in her, but after some time the sad tide ebbed away. She did not attach those hours of ache to a story of self: "I waited so long to wed and how unfair..." or "I am a widow, everything is over." Similarly, she attached no story when her lung was removed, and though she felt very fragile and for six weeks had to be careful to have no one hug her, she was not overly bothered by it. Actually, it was kind of an adventure.

Nora observes that some people, and not only in Crestone, are emerging from their birth or adopted religious tradition into a more spacious spirituality. For herself, she enjoys the ritual and mystery of traditional Catholicism as much as she ever did, but she no longer needs them. The solitude still attracts her and the spiritual exercises still move her, yet if occasionally she finds herself in, say, a bar and drinking a whiskey, it is not so vastly different, really.

Rung Nine: Exits Become Entrances

EXEMPLARS: FATHER DAVE DENNY; TSOKNYI RINPOCHE

"Do you know what the opposite of spirituality is?" Father Dave asked me. His answer surprised me: "Ideology." When feeling inadequate or suffering a sense of deprivation, people often retreat into ideology or dogma, sometimes catastrophically. The further Father Dave has gone in contemplation (a Christian form of meditation), though, the less need he has even for Christian ideology to overcome despair or hardships. For him hardship or despair no longer tells the end of the story.

The exit: Dave left the common world of daily pleasantry behind when his mother developed Alzheimer's, not even sure as he faithfully tended her that she knew who he was. The entrance: That heartbreak, sad and sadder, also pushed him into a realm sweet and dear. As he unstintingly cared for his mother he experienced, perhaps for the first time, unconditional, limitless love for someone — the exact opposite of what their roles had been when he was a baby. Father Dave certainly does not ferret out misfortune, but when forbearance and contemplative gentleness are brought to bear, the tragic side of life, too, can pave a route to his spiritual goals.

Thus Father Dave has exited Thoreau's mass of men who lead lives of quiet desperation. Perhaps most of us have simply grown used to that state, and it would feel strange if life didn't feel slightly strange. Tsoknyi Rinpoche, even more so than Dave, has trained so thoroughly in mind-at-ease practices, however — in *carefree dignity* (as he titled one book) — that lighthearted grace and ease under pressure have become second nature to him. If suddenly, out of the blue, he experiences disturbance, then, as with Dave during contemplation, it registers with a jolt. That sudden shock of internal discomfort wakes him like an alarm clock going off and reminds him not to give total credence to that troubling thought. Once this process of disquiet-becomes-clarity becomes automatic, one is on the road to enlightenment, and probably Father Dave or Tsoknyi Rinpoche could not detour off it, even if they tried.

The linguist Noam Chomsky observed that, just as we cannot expect a cat to do algebra, why believe that limited human intelligence can grasp the ultimate laws of the universe? Like an ant swept off a pair of trousers by an unperceived hand, so we feeble mortals are tossed by mysterious unseen forces we cannot fully fathom. (Well, that hand was the old idea of God, wasn't it?) Not enlightenment but the step preceding it may consist of intuitively living in harmony with what omniscience would know, without, however, our knowing it. Though the people featured in this book do not claim to know ultimate truth, some of them may nonetheless embody portions of it.

There is Yochi, contentedly living in nature, in summery days and in freezing days, owning scarcely a possession. Always in good humor, Tsoknyi Rinpoche requires no fixed residence, for his home consists of helping those who cry out (aloud or silently). Nora Schreiber and Howie Ostler inhabit an inner spaciousness more commodious than any outward dwelling could be. And so it goes, this catalog of Crestonians who live in a different and sometimes better way. That way can be as simple as Mark Elliott's putting others first. Or as unusual as Ralph and Megumi savoring a subtle one taste, making palatable most experiences. A first whiff of enlightenment may be detected when, like Kate Steichen, you attempt to be grateful for whatever happens. Would all these above aspects of grace — if united in a single mind and body — add up to ideal being?

Enlightenment may be simply: seeing everything as sacred, converting the mundane into the numinous. And some in Crestone at least try to do that. Ossian, for example, views unlikely things — like the kitschy picture of Jesus found in the town Free Box — as blessed. When Neil Hogan asks the *nagas* (snakelike protector-spirits) for permission before he pees by the stream, even if there are no *nagas*, he is establishing a sacramental relation to the land. If this Earth is, against the odds, to remain a congenial and habitable abode, it cannot be reduced to a material ball that can be privately owned and exploited. The small minority who gaze with awe and wonder on it may need to deepen their vision and grow in number. A sustainable and even enlightened planet becomes conceivable when more people are like Bertha in Crestone, who proclaim their spiritual affiliation: "My religion? I am standing on it."

A Note on Dates

This book was written over a longer period of time than
a book should take, from 2007 through 2016, to be
exact. Early on, I fantasized about pulling off Thoreau's sleight of hand in *Walden*, when, for readability and pith,
he compressed two years in the woods into one. But two years
are not nine, and a woods usually varies less from year to year
than a town does, even a small one halfway from anywhere.

Yet Crestone did change, even in the short period covered
in this book. When I began writing, for instance, cell phones
and the internet were dicey propositions here, requiring the
favor of the gods, rather arthritic gods, but now they rip and
zip and zoom along, as though to Silicon Valley born. Even
Crestone's few indispensable businesses proved not immune
to mortality. Feeding folks here for two generations, Curt's
grocery was seemingly the one irreplaceable institution in
Crestone, but then the Mercantile opened, offering lower
prices, and Curt's was no more. The Bliss Café, where some
scenes recounted here transpired — well, don't go looking
for it, it now has a new owner and a new name. And Crestone Telecom — "the baby Jesus of telecommunications" —
has merged to become Colorado Central Telecom, though

Ralph's quiet ambition remains: employees should get more than a salary but personal growth as well.

The town's cast of characters alters, too, as even community stalwarts like David and Lorain Fox Davis move away, often for health reasons. The change I liked least was that, as mentioned earlier, late in the book's time span dear Bertha Gotterup died. (Yet in these pages she posthumously inhabits the present tense, for she was alive, as vital as anybody or more so, when I was writing about her.) Also, when I began, Tsoknyi Rinpoche had recently lived here, his home was still here, and his organization Pundarika was (and still is) headquartered here: coming and going regularly, he was very much a presence in Crestone. Today he arrives, leads his annual retreat, and darts away again, while another rinpoche of equal stature, Dzigar Kongtrul, has relocated here. Were I beginning today, Dzigar Kongtrul would of necessity replace Tsoknyi in the lineup, and I wonder how different a book this would have been.

Still, the avalanche of rapid change uprooting much that is time-honored elsewhere has not buried the Crestone told of in these pages. Most of the drama and comedy reported here could with equal plausibility have transpired in any year of this narrative — or happen still. (The words *now* or *recently* in the text refer to actions transpiring concurrently with or slightly before their being written down.) If an event in Crestone could have taken place only under time-specific or singular circumstances I have cited the year or month; otherwise, I did not burden the reader with keeping track of not overly relevant dates.

Enlightenment Town is a photograph of Crestone in a time roughly called "today" or "now." Yet at a certain point the book, should it survive, will fade into a historic keepsake, nostalgia replacing familiarity.

Second Dedication

To the Dear Ones:

Leon and Blanche and Sam Paine, and all the ten children of Jacob and Jenny

Katherine Rankin

Brad Evans

Carol Kleinmaier

Katie Morris, loveliest among mortals

Suzzanne and Ruth Ann, who helped me keep body and mind well enough to write this book

Zen Dr. Rabbi Scott, just right, just so
Mechthild Amerongen

Sri Margot Born

Professor Candland of Muslim charities fame

Kendra

Karen and Phil

LPS and LSP

Nancy Goldring, exquisite and valiant artist

Mrs. Goreau

Kenny Dessain (Wiley Coyote)

James Delano

Andeeeeeeee Blum!

The Susans: Hadler, Nugent,
Ginsberg, and Peterson

Debbie

Bettina Irma

Dick Ostman and Michael Paine, missed, gone too soon

Cousin Paula and Coco

The Old Hotel Brouwer

Hans Oudmaijer

James Donald McGregor,
coeditor of the *Paine & McGregor News*

Dr. Alistair Kelly Morris Jr. and
Coco

RGK (Goldie)

Jay Tolson

Hi HI: Virginia, Lee, and Jeff

The German painter Thomas Rohnacher

· Bon-bon-la

Sandy Friedman

REL'62 (JD, AW, HS, KT)

Anam Thubten

and whomever I'm forgetting

With appreciation to: Jason Gardner, Bill Gladstone,
and Ms. Macko

About the Author

Jeffery Paine is best known for bringing Eastern culture and spirituality to popular audiences in the West. He is the author of *Re-enchantment: Tibetan Buddhism Comes to the West* and *Father India: How Encounters with an Ancient Culture Transformed the Modern West*. His other works include *The Poetry of Our World*, an anthology he edited with Nobel Prize winner Joseph Brodsky, and the anthology *Adventures with the Buddha*. He also wrote Huston Smith's memoir *Tales of Wonder*.

Paine holds a PhD in intellectual history from Princeton University. He was the literary editor of the *Wilson Quarterly* at the Woodrow Wilson International Center for Scholars at the Smithsonian, contributing editor of the *San Francisco Review of Books*, a judge of the Pulitzer Prize, and vice president of the National Book Critics Circle. He has taught or been a guest professor at Princeton University, San Francisco State University, Volksuniversiteit Amsterdam, and University of Minnesota.

In addition to his books, Paine has written for major publications including the *New York Times*, the *Washington Post*, the *Chicago Tribune*, the *New Republic*, the *Boston Globe*, the *Los Angeles Times*, *US News and World Report*, the *Nation*, and the *Wall Street Journal*. He has frequently appeared on C-SPAN, NPR, and other radio and TV programs and has spoken at the Smithsonian, the Library of Congress, ICA (London), and universities around the country.